# A Plague on the World

Robert Ley
and
Hans-Georg Otto

# A Plague on the World

Robert Ley
and
Hans-Georg Otto

Clemens & Blair, LLC
— 2024 —

CLEMENS & BLAIR, LLC

Clemens & Blair, LLC, is a non-profit educational publisher.
www.clemensandblair.com

**Library of Congress Cataloging-in-Publication Data**

Ley, Robert and Otto, Hans-Georg: *A Plague on the World*
Translation of *Pesthauch Der Welt* (R. Ley, 1944) and
    *Der Jude als Weltparasit* (H.-G. Otto, 1943).

p. cm.
Includes bibliographical references

**ISBN 978-1963-1430-89**
(pbk.: alk. paper)

1. National Socialism
2. Jewish Question, the
3. History of Jews in Germany

Printing number: 9 8 7 6 5 4 3 2 1

Printed in the United States of America on acid-free paper.

# ACKNOWLEDGMENT

The editor would like to acknowledge the excellent translation work by Ms. Mildred Grau for Book II; her efforts are much appreciated. Also, the outstandingly restored and colorized graphics in Book I are the products of a talented digital artist, Robert Penman, working from black-and-white German originals; his contribution is invaluable.

# CONTENTS

# INTRODUCTION
## THOMAS DALTON

The world today faces many grave problems, but arguably the gravest and most urgent is what has long been called the Jewish Question: how society should respond to the presence of a wealthy, powerful, and malicious Jewish minority. This question—or 'problem,' as the case may be —has existed for as long as Jews have interacted with Gentile populations, that is, for literally thousands of years. For millennia, prominent observers have viewed the Jews as a plague, a curse, upon the Earth. The situation is the same, or worse, in the present day.

The earliest mention of the Jewish people dates back to around 1350 BC, in the Amarna Letters to Pharoah Akhenaten. In one letter, a local ruler complains of "war waged against me" by the "Habiru" people, whom some scholars have identified as Hebrews. In the carved stone tablet known as the Merneptah Stelle, circa 1200 BC, "Israel" is cited as an evidently belligerent tribe that suffered a great defeat; and a comparable stone of 850 BC records a defeat of the militant "House of David." We also have many Old Testament stories of Jews involved with numerous wars, insurrections, and mass murders of their non-Jewish neighbors.

Over subsequent centuries, we have many documented views of the Jews as hostile to foreigners, misanthropic, cruel, and bloodthirsty—to a degree exceptional among all known peoples. Thus, we are unsurprised to learn that, in 41 AD, Roman emperor Claudius issued an edict rebuking the Jews of Alexandria, accusing them of "fomenting a general plague which infests the whole world".[1] There we have it, explicitly, for the first time in history: *the Jews are a plague upon the world.*

It is hardly shocking, then, to learn that leading National Socialists of Hitler's Germany felt the same way. They well knew that, in the intervening 2,000 years since the time of Claudius, that the Jewish threat had only grown in severity and urgency. Distinguished observers repeatedly condemned the Hebrews: "an accursed race" (Seneca), "implacable hatred of mankind" (Tacitus), "a den of devils" (Martin Luther), "a republic

---

[1] For details, see T. Dalton, *Eternal Strangers* (2020; Castle Hill).

of cunning usurers" (Johann Herder), "deadly to the human race" (Voltaire), "great master of lies" (Schopenhauer), and "plastic demons of decay" (Richard Wagner). By the late 1700s, some Germans, such as Herder, had taken to calling the Jews "parasites":

> [This] people of God…have been, for thousands of years, nay, almost from their beginning, parasitical plants on the trunks of other nations.

Some 50 years later, French socialist Pierre Proudhon described Judaism as a "mercantile and usurious parasitism," adding: "the Jew remains a Jew, a parasitic race." Schopenhauer echoed this sentiment, stating that the Jewish race "lives parasitically on other nations and their soil." In 1871, Russian anarchist Mikhail Bakunin expressed some blunt thoughts on "this whole Jewish world, which constitutes a single exploiting sect, a sort of bloodsucker people, a collective parasite." In his notebooks of 1885, Nietzsche wrote that "the Jewish soul [tries] to gain a foothold in a parasitic manner." In his *Antichrist*, he adds that the Jewish priest is "a parasitical type of man".[2]

In his *Mein Kampf* of 1925, Hitler recalled and expanded upon this longstanding criticism. He wrote:

> People who can sneak their way into the human body poli-tic and, like parasites, make others work for them, can form a state without possessing any specific territory. This is chiefly applicable to that parasitic nation which, today more than ever, preys upon the honest portion of mankind: the Jews. (vol 1, 4.12)

> The Jew, however, hasn't the slightest trace of idealism. He has never been a nomad, but always a parasite in the body of other peoples. If he occasionally abandoned regions where he had previously lived, he didn't do so voluntarily. He did it because, from time to time, he was driven out by those whom he had abused. Jewish self-expansion is a

---

[2] For all above quotations, see again *Eternal Strangers* for source details.

typical parasitic phenomenon; he always seeks new feeding ground for his race. (vol 1, 11.11)

[The Jew] is and remains an eternal parasite, a sponger who, like a pernicious bacillus, spreads over wider and wider areas as they become favorable to him. The effect produced by his presence is also like that of a sponger; wherever he establishes himself, the host people die out, sooner or later. (ibid.)

The man who thinks that he can bind himself by treaty with [Jewish] parasites is like a tree that believes it can form a profitable agreement with mistletoe. (vol 2, 14.12)

Joseph Goebbels reiterated this view in his personal diaries. In the entry dated 13 May 1943, he reflected on a question:

Why are there any Jews in the world order? That would be exactly like asking, Why are there potato bugs? Nature is dominated by the law of struggle. There will always be parasites...[3]

Upon entry into war in September 1939, such ideas were no longer theoretical; they were concrete and potentially deadly. Jews in Bolshevist Russia were a looming threat to the east, capitalist Jews in England and France to the west were activated against Germany, and internally, thousands of German Jews agitated for the downfall of Hitler's government. Hitler was thus faced by belligerent Jews on all sides: left, right, and center. And American Jews were also gearing up for war—all because one leader and his people sought to live independent of the global Jewish matrix of total control.

*****

Into this active war-setting stepped a number of German scholars, in an attempt to document the Jewish threat, to educate the people, and to offer

---

[3] See *Goebbels on the Jews* (2019; Castle Hill).

an intellectual defense of Germany's ideology. One of the brightest and best-educated men of the NS hierarchy was Robert Ley (1890-1945). Born into a working-class household, he attended college at Jena, served with distinction in World War One, and eventually earned a PhD in chemistry in 1920. Ley joined the National Socialist party in 1925, becoming a loyal follower of Hitler. In Cologne in 1928, he established an NS newspaper, *Westdeutscher Beobachter*, focusing on anti-Jewish themes and stories. Rising quickly through the party ranks, Ley was named *Reichsleiter* in mid-1933—the second highest civilian rank in the party.

Owing to his working-class background, Ley was assigned to develop German labor policy via the newly-formed German Labor Front (DAF). He played a major role in the establishment of the "Strength Through Joy" initiative which was very popular among German workers. Ley managed to retain Hitler's support throughout the war, serving as one of the Führer's 'inner circle.'

Though not active in either military or Jewish policy, Ley spoke out vehemently against Reich enemies, particularly the Jews. Should Germany lose, he said, "Funeral pyres would be built on which the Jews would burn us"—prophetic, given the many Allied fire-bombings late in the war. After the war, Ley was captured and held for trial at Nuremberg, but managed to commit suicide prior to the start of proceedings.

In early 1944, with the war going badly, Ley was tasked with writing a concise booklet documenting the case against the Jews and portraying them as a literal plague upon the Earth. It was intended as a populist book, for a wide audience, rather than a typical academic tome. Short, to the point, factually accurate, and lightened with clever cartoons and drawings—these were to be the chief characteristics. As a particularly strident critic of the Jews—remarkable, given the milieu—Ley was the right man for the job. He was well-known for his striking attacks, including such essays as "International Melting Pot or United Nation-States of Europe?" in 1941.[4] In short order, he issued a text entitled *Pesthauch der Welt*—A Plague on the World. This text, fully reproduced here, constitutes Book I of the present volume.

---

[4] For the full essay, see T. Dalton (ed.), *Classic Essays on the Jewish Question* (2022; Clemens & Blair).

As stated, notable in this small booklet were a number of cartoon sketches by an unnamed artist. The style is reminiscent of the more famous drawings for *Der Stürmer* done by the man known as Fips, though none of these cartoons are signed or initialed.[5] Be that as it may, contemporary digital artist Robert Penman has restored and, for the first time, colorized these images that appeared in the 1944 German original. They provide a graphic and wryly-humorous supplement to Ley's devastating text.

Book II of the present volume—"The Jew as World-Parasite"—was written somewhat earlier, in 1943, by an obscure individual named Hans-Georg Otto. Almost nothing is known of him, other than that he evidently worked under the direction of Alfred Rosenberg on the mission of NS ideological research and education. Otto wrote two preceding booklets, "Battle of Destiny in the East" and "Europe and America," which established the groundwork for the subject essay. Otto's writing is careful, articulate, and properly cited; he was apparently not a scholar on the level of Ley or Rosenberg, but he was clearly a capable and competent researcher and writer.

Both writings here are exceptional, though, owing to their explicit and targeted attacks on the Jews, and to their timing; by mid-1943, it was clear that things were turning against the Germans, and pressure surely began to mount—not only on the Front but also back home, among the scholars and intellectuals who were now urgently called upon to aid the war effort. These two texts stand as classic works of the genre, and provide immense educational value—both on the thinking of that time and in light of present events in today's world. These two works, like much of National Socialist writing, embody timeless lessons and eternal wisdom, for those willing to listen objectively.

---

[5] For many excellent examples of Fips' work, see volumes one and two of *Pan-Judah!* (2021; 2022; Clemens & Blair), with original artwork restored and colorized by Robert Penman.

# BOOK ONE

---

# "A Plague on the World"

by
Robert Ley

*A Plague on the World*

# THE ETERNAL JEW

The Second World War is a battle between worldviews, and the side with the strongest faith will be victorious. Only he who is convinced of the justice of his cause, and who in fact has justice on his side, who acts reasonably and correctly, and who recognizes and follows the laws of nature, can have the strongest faith.

All natural life is eternal battle, and battle is the father of all things. Battle, however, is possible only between two opposing poles and powers. Mankind has named these battling worlds "good" and "evil," "God" and "Satan," "noble" and "crude," "construction and destruction," "life" or "death." These are all ways of saying that nature is a constant process of coming and going, a constant transformation of forces and materials. Science has a chemical and physical law that says: Nothing perishes; everything is constantly changing. Whatever we call it, whether we use the words of science or say it in a more primitive way, the eternal, inescapable law is that *life means battle*, that battle comes from competing energies, and that something new comes from their meeting.

This knowledge is one of the fundamental principles of National Socialism, a principle on which it acts. We maintain that human society, government, economics, and culture come from the harmony of common blood and a common race, and that the antipole of humanity is the Jew, who embodies the competing race. National Socialist thinking is therefore anti-Semitic, since it fights the Jew not from religious reasons, but rather only from its racial knowledge, from the depths of its worldview, for it knows that the peoples cannot live as racial communities if they do not defend themselves against the Jew. The Jew is the enemy not only in his personal form, but rather even more in the Jewish mentality and in the Jewish approach to the world.

The National Socialist worldview should better be called the National Socialist understanding of the world! It is not a philosophical construction to help the individual understand the world, to give him a place to stand, but rather it is the knowledge, it is the facts, of how the world really is, independent of the standpoint of an observer. What we see as race and blood, and what we battle as the great enemy of this blood, is based not merely on our opinion, but rather on scientifically-proven knowledge.

Everything in nature obeys ancient and unchangeable laws. Nothing happens apart from these natural laws. The laws strive toward harmony and construction. Every natural creature must obey some of these countless laws. It has a mission, thereby obeying its drives, its instincts, and its understanding. The opposite of harmony is chaos and disharmony. If racial community displays harmony in blood and nature, the Jew is the chaotic, disharmonic factor in such human harmony. National Socialism wants to release energy by promoting communities of race and blood so that humanity can develop its abilities and virtues to the highest level. National Socialism thus strives for the highest level of culture. It respects beauty and joy, health and human satisfaction, strength, development, and progress. Each of these is insufficient by itself without the will to defend this ideal from the danger of chaos and destruction. Thus, the first question we must ask to fulfill our National Socialist ideal is this: *Who is the Jew?* He who does not understand the Jewish Question, who does not study and fully understand it, will not understand the world, its development, and its battles.

Who is the Jew? The Jew is also a product of his drives, and obeys his natural law. The Führer calls this "Lucifer's tragedy"! That is so! In nature, we call destructive elements 'parasites.' They are creatures who can no longer survive on their own, due to the atrophy of their vital organs, such as their lungs, digestive system, or reproductive organs. They are no longer able to secure their own food and digest it, and are therefore dependent on other living plants or animals. They devour their hosts. They fall like locusts on them, suck their life away, destroy them. Their tragedy is that, in doing so, they destroy themselves in the end. Nature always helps. When parasites gain the upper hand, they devour each other.

The Jew is just such a parasite!

The Jew developed like any other parasite. Parasites develop through unnatural inbreeding and by the inheritance of the worst traits. Parasites develop under some sort of natural pressure, through unnatural, perverse inheritance, through forced atrophy—in other words, as the result of disease, bad environment, and inheritance. The Jew is such a creature, given his origins, development, and biological nature.

The Jew was earlier concentrated in the Middle East. Since at that time there were no railroads, steamships, or airplanes, it was the natural center of world commerce, situated between Europe, Asia, and Africa. It was the place where the White man from the cities of the North Sea and the Baltic Sea went to trade with Negroes from Africa and the inhabitants of Asia. Inevitably, a racial swamp developed, formed from the three major and entirely different parts of humanity.

*The Jew Promises Paradise*

The laws of genetics teach us that nature does not want those of mixed race, tolerating them only if some parts atrophy or become strained. Mestizos and Mulattos are infertile, and only under exceptional circumstances can cretins bear offspring. The racial swamp that Palestine became had a central position in world finance and commerce. It was the place where Asia, Africa, and Europe met. As a result, the worst type of mixed race developed. Over the course of millennia, Caucasian mountain tribes drove the racial trash into the desert, as Jewish history records, and there sealed them off hermetically. Through biological processes, this mixed race from three continents developed, through incest, into parasites of the first order. There is no doubt that, according to botanic and zoological laws, the Jew is a true and genuine parasite.

The racially healthy person has one blood in his veins, while he of mixed race has several blood types. Over the millennia, the Jew's blood became distorted and ruined. What does that mean? Science teaches that the properties of various materials, such as glass, wood, iron, etc., differ only in that they are made of different molecules, or different building blocks. Both the outward form and the inner structure can be different. A molecule is made of many atoms, the smallest possible entity. These atoms spin around a molecular core. The molecules differ according to the number of atoms, and through the nature of the spin and the speed of the constituent atoms. To understand genetics, we must understand two principles:

1. A bastard with two different types of blood does not have a new type of blood, rather both different blood types remain within the bastard. They move together in his veins, which explains the bastard's limitations.

2. Mendel's laws state that bastards move back to their original nature or race. According to Mendel's laws, bastards of the same type change from a ratio of 1:1 to 2. that is: The offspring of two similar bastards comes 1/4 from the one, 1/4 from the other, but 2/4 is bastard.

By the third or fourth generation at the latest, the offspring have returned to their racial origins. This law, however, applies only to related entities. The offspring of widely different races, such as black-white, red-white, red-black, etc., do not return to their original racial makeup, rather become Mestizos or Mulattos that are either infertile or, due to isolation and incest, develop into parasitic creatures. In parasites, the constituent elements, the molecules and building blocks, are torn apart and destroyed, and only fragments of what was originally there remain. This explains why the parasite is driven to the host from which he descended, and why he must suck the life from it. Thus, the Jew, who has become a human parasite, must return to the peoples from whom he descended, and this produce of the racial swamp of the Middle East must live off them.

It is clear that the amount of destruction in a Jew varies. There are Jews with less damaged blood, and others whose blood is entirely fragmented. Thus there are some Jews who only value profit, and live from exploiting their host peoples. Other Jews are in a more degenerate biological state, and seek to mate with the women and men of their host people. Finally there is a third sort of Jew that is entirely decayed; it values ritual murder, which means that its drives lead it to drink the blood of its host peoples.

The biologic laws that govern the Jewish parasite make it the antirace of humanity, its antipole, and his drives form the common bond of criminality and sickness that connects all Jews of the world together more firmly than is possible through mere human laws, words, or rules. Thus: All Jews work together, and all Jews are depraved and criminal.

When talking with Dietrich Eckart, the Führer once said:

> What you once wrote is probably true. One can only understand the Jew when one knows what his final goal is: *To control the world in order to destroy the world*. He believes he must dominate all of humanity to, as he claims, establish paradise on earth. Only he can do that, he imagines. But even in the means he chooses, one can see that it will lead him to a different end. Although claiming to lead humanity to the heights, he torments it into a state of desperation, into insanity, into collapse. If he is not stopped, he destroys them. He is driven to that, although he dimly realizes it will mean his own destruction. He can do nothing else; he is forced into it.
>
> The chief cause of his hatred, I think, is his realization that he depends on the existence of his victim. He has to destroy someone, while realizing that that inevitably means his own destruction. You might call it: The tragedy of Lucifer.

*The Battle of Good Against Evil*

# —2—
# JUDAISM IS RUIN, DESTRUCTION, DECAY, AND MURDER!

Jewry, flowing from biological laws, is best expressed in its religion and its conception of god. God represents the highest ideal for peoples and for humanity, so how people conceive of god reveals how they think, their spiritual nature. Yahweh, the Jewish god, is a god of revenge, of cursing, of destruction, one who rains sulfur and brimstone down on humanity, who thunders at them, whose lightning sets fields and meadows ablaze. Yahweh is the grim Jewish god who exists only to give Jews profits, much gold and money, and lordship over Gentiles.

There is nothing cruder than the Jewish religious books: the Talmud, the *Shulchan Aruch*,[1] the books of Moses,[2] and of the prophets. Since he does not even trust his god, the Jew sets the "rabbi" above Yahweh and declares the Jewish god Jehovah must study the laws written down by the rabbis in the Torah in order to rule the world. The whole is a collection of ghost hunting and mysticism, blind cursing and the crassest egotism, an unimaginable superiority complex, sick perversity, the overturning of all natural laws, lust for murder, terror, and horror.

But let us listen to the Jew himself. We see how dangerous the Jew thinks his doctrines are, and how eager he is to see that they remain unknown to Gentiles. In the Yalkut Hadash, Nr. 72, we read: "It is forbidden for a Gentile to discover the secrets of our doctrines; should a Gentile discover them, it is as if he laid waste to the entire world and denied the holy name (Yahweh)".[3]

Capitalism was born from fatalism. Calvin, one of the most important Jewish hirelings, says: "He who is poor must remain poor, and he

---

[1] For a concise analysis of the Talmud and the Shulchan Aruch, see Erich Bischoff, *The Book of the Shulchan Aruch* (2023; Clemens & Blair).

[2] That is, the Torah: Genesis, Exodus, Leviticus, Numbers, and Deuteronomy.

[3] Compare with Sanhedrin 59a2: "And Rabbi Yohanan says: A Gentile who engages in Torah study is liable to receive the death penalty."

who is rich must make more money. It is a sin to teach otherwise." The Jew says: "All is determined in advance" (Pirkei Avot 111).

*The Jew as Pseudo-Artist*

There is no end to the Jew's superiority complex. It can only be seen as insane. Let us listen to these crazy words:

- "Each Jew must tell himself that the world was created for me" (Sanhedrin 37a16).

- "The land of Israel was created first, then the rest of the world... The land of Israel was watered by the rains, the rest of the world with what was left" (Taanit 10a2).

- "For each who saves the life of a Jewish soul, it is as if he had saved the entire world" (Bava Batra 11a, Sanhedrin 37a13).[4]

- "Everywhere the Jews come, they will become the lords of their masters" (Sanhedrin 104a15).

Reading that, who does not think of Roosevelt, Churchill, and Stalin.

The proud Jew further says: "All Jews are the children of nobility" (Shabbat 67a10, 11a, 128; Bava Metzia 113b12).

Who should be surprised at such arrogance when one recalls that even Gentiles are always talking about the "Chosen People." And it is true: they *are* chosen…for lies, vulgarity, fraud, murder, and sloth.

Let us listen once more to the Jewish law books:

- Jewish perjury: "If a Jew wishes to annul all his oaths of the previous year, he must say at the beginning of the new year: 'All the oaths that I swore are invalid'" (Nedarim 23b1).

- And again: "For the sake of peace, one may change his words a bit" (Yevamot 65b8).

- Jewish cunning: "May the righteous (the Jews) be cunning? Yes! With the pure (the Jews) you are pure, with others (Gentiles) the opposite."

- Jewish vulgarity: "Gentiles are to be seen as unclean from birth" (Shabbat 16b9, 17a4; Avodah Zarah 36b2, Niddah 31b).

- "All Gentiles are whores" (Shulchan aruch, Even Ha-ezer 6, 8).

- "He who has slept with a Gentile has slept with a whore" (Sanhedrin 82a; Avodah Zarah 36b12).

---

[4] It adds: "anyone who destroys one Jewish soul, it is as if he destroyed an entire world."

- "The marriage of Gentiles is the same as sleeping with animals" (Sanhedrin 74b Tosahot).

These are a few choice passages of Jewish lust and vulgarity. One could continue such filthy citations indefinitely, each one worse than the one before, a mixture of perversity, a sick superiority complex, and the basest sentiments.

Let us continue with other amoral characteristics of the Jew, as revealed in his law books:

- Jewish insolence: "The home of a Gentile is like a barn" (Eruvin 62a3, 72b).

- "Gentiles are not human beings" (Yevamot 61a1 Tosahot).

- "May Gentiles be called human beings? No! For it is written (Ezekiel 34:31): 'You Jews are human beings, you are called humans, but Gentiles are not called human beings, but animals'" (Bava Metzia 114b2).[5]

- "Only the Jews are important in the world. They are the wheat, the Gentiles the chaff" (Isaak Abrabanul, Commentary on Isaiah, Jeremiah, Ezekiel and the 12 minor prophets....).

This insolence reaches its epitome in the following citation. One can hardly believe it:

- "God created the Gentiles in human form, although they are animals... But he created them to serve the Jews day and night, never to cease. It is not right for Jews to be served by animals in the form of animals, but rather by animals in the form of human beings" (Midrash Talpiot, p. 255, Warsaw edition, 1875).

---

[5] Compare to Yevamot 98a3; Berakhot 58a15. See also Ezekiel 23:20, where the genitals of non-Jews are compared to those of donkeys.

This is arrogance so impudent, so outrageous, that it is insane. That is why the Jew alone is the father of class struggle.

*The Jew as a Parasite and Freeloader*

But let us listen some more:

- Jewish fraud: "One may lend money to Gentiles at usurious rates." (Bava Metzia 71a1.).

- "The Jew should always speak in a way that makes him look innocent" (Pesachim 3a13).

- "What is the role of the Jew on the earth? To appear stupid" (Chullin 89a10).

- "As soon as the Jews learn wisdom, they also become sly" (Sotah 21b2).

- Jewish theft and Jewish exploitation: "Yahweh will not forgive a Jew who returns a lost item to a Gentile" (Sanhedrin 76b2).

- "If a house has been rented to a Gentile, anything found in it belongs to the Jew who finds it, even if it is in the middle of the house" (Bava Metzia 26).

- "If a Jew finds money in a place frequented by many people, it belongs to him because its owner has lost it; the Jew, after all, does not know that someone has lost it" (Bava Metzia 21b).

- "Theft, robbery, the kidnapping of a beautiful women, etc., is forbidden if it is done by a Gentile to another Gentile, or by a Gentile to a Jew, but may be done by a Jew to a Gentile" (Sanhedrin 57a14).

- "The Jewish soul lusts after robbery and sexual crimes" (Chagigah 11b19).

Workers, listen to this:

- "If a Jew hires a worker, he should pay the lowest possible wage" (Bava Metzia 87a18). Or: "Robbing a Gentile is permitted. If robbery is permitted, how much more is it permitted to rob a wage-earner" (Bava Metzia 87b18).

- "Bribe Gentile judges before they sign the judgment" (Gittin 28b10).

The Jew both bribes and allows himself to be bribed. Listen to what the Jew said about justice:

- "When a Jew and a Gentile appear before the court, rule in favor of the Jew if you can, using Jewish law. Say to the Gentile:

'That is what our law says.' When you can rule in favor of the Jew on the basis of Gentile law, tell the Gentile: 'That is what your own law says.' When neither is possible, defeat the Gentile by trickery" (Bava Kamma 113a21).

The Jew is the laziest creature. Listen to what the Jew himself says:

- "Work is torture" (Taanit 12b12).

- "You Jews to not need to get up early, to go to bed late, and to eat bread won by your sweat, for Yahweh gives to his Jews even while they sleep" (Yoma 77a6).[6]

This highly immoral attitude toward labor is entirely consistent with the capitalistic opinions, and the lust for profit and exploitation, of the Jew.
In conclusion, listen to the Jew as murderer and war criminal:

- "Gentiles should be ruined, but the Jews should rejoice" (Bava Metzia 33b5).

- "Shedding blood is punishable when committed by a Gentile against another Gentile, or for a Gentile against a Jew, but there is no penalty if it is done by a Jew to a Gentile" (Sanhedrin 57a14).

- "Kill the best of the Gentiles" (Tractate Soferim 15,10; Midrash Tanchuma, Beschalach 8,1)

- "Each who sheds the blood of the Gentiles brings a sacrifice to Yahweh" (Simon Darschan, Jalgut Schimoni).

This murderous and criminal standpoint leads to the Jewish attitude toward war:

---

[6] See also: Psalms 127:2.

- "It is permitted to incite the world's Gentiles into war" (Berakhot 7b, Megillah 6b).

- "When you march to war, do not be the first, but rather the last, so that you may also be the first to return home" (Pesachim 113a10).

I believe that this is enough to show the amoral nature of the Jew. The Jew knows no morality, no decency, and he has no conscience. He is the parasitic antipole of humanity.

If anyone wishes further proof for the genuinely parasitic nature of Jewry, he should ask whether or not the Jews have ever created a culture, an economy, or a state of their own. Can anyone find a single Jew anywhere who, in any field whatever, has shown creative, original abilities? I know that Jewish propaganda has been trying for millennia to find this proof. Whenever a Jew somewhere or another shows some superficial talent, the whole Jewish mess tries to make such superficial talent into real talent in order to prove that the Jews, too, can be creative. However, when anyone looks behind such Jewish machinations, he will easily be able to prove that the ostensible Jewish creations are actually stolen, plagiarized, or borrowed from somewhere else.

Even the claim that in ancient times the Jews had their own state, which the Zionists today use to support their claim for a new state, is false. There was a Middle Eastern ghetto in Jerusalem and its surroundings, but it hardly united all the Jews in the Middle East. We know that there were many more Jews living in Babylon, Egypt, Greece, and on the Greek islands, than there were in Jerusalem. And when we investigate this presumed Jewish state more closely, we learn from history that there were constant rebellions and counter-rebellions. One priest fought another priest. There was eternal unrest and rebellion throughout the ancient era, and into the Roman Empire. The myth of a Jewish state is as much a lie as all the other Jewish claims of their accomplishments.

However, in one area one must grant that the Jews have the greatest gifts. No other people on Earth is more gifted in criminality, in lies, in theft, in exploitation, and in corruption than the Jew.

The Jew can behave no differently, because he is by nature born to crime. It is his fateful drive: "The tragedy of Lucifer!" All Jews are so inclined, one a little more, another a little less. Crime binds them together. That does not build a Jewish community, for that would be a positive trait. Quite the opposite. One must see how the Jew cheats, exploits, and tortures his blood comrades when he is placed in power over them. There is no worse traitor to his own blood than the Jew. I myself have seen how Jewish overlords misuse their Jewish comrades and exploit them to death.

—3—

# NO TRACE OF A SENSE OF COMMUNITY

Anyone who watches Jews trade between themselves can see how Jews treat each other. There is no trace of loyalty or trust to be found. They cheat each other just as they cheat Gentiles.

This becomes evident only when others have power over the Jew and he can no longer escape his fate. As long as he thinks he can conceal things with some success behind the Jewish mask, he will do so. There is no stronger bond than that which joins criminals. One Jew protects the other, at least to the outside world, regardless of the distance between them, or whatever social differences may exist between them. The Jew in America protects the Jew in Poland, Moscow, or Berlin, the rich Jew protects the poor Jew, and the poor Jew protects the rich Jew. The outward differences in religion, whether one is strongly religious or half religious, Zionist or non-Zionist, all these make no difference at all. When it comes to concealing a Jewish crime from the Gentiles, thereby concealing the true nature of Jewry from the Gentiles, Jews throughout the whole world join together and use every method to protect and defend their Jewish racial comrades.

Here one can really say: All Jews stand by each other, and are ready to swear to any perjury, to bribe with as much money as is needed, to use all methods at their disposal, to stand by each other. This fact proves the Jewish drive for self-preservation: the Jew knows that when one of his racial comrades is revealed, Jewry as a whole is revealed.

That was true in ancient days as much as today. The Jewish grain-speculator Joseph in Egypt brought his whole rotten family there so that they could share his power and exploit the Egyptians.[7] Young Moses gathered all the strength he could to protect every last Jew from the just persecution of the Egyptians.

The Jewish habit of protecting each other became most clear whenever some Jew or another committed ritual murder. Just one of many examples: The rich Jew Adolphe Cremieux from Paris used his large

---

[7] See Genesis 37-48.

fortune to conceal the ritual murder of a Catholic priest in Damascus. He bribed the caliph of Egypt. Although the appellate court had confirmed all the details, just as had the original court, files were destroyed to remove any trace of this Jewish crime.

In the modern era, the Jews have established major world organizations to conceal their criminal deeds, which are joined together under Freemasonry. World Freemasonry, which has gradually recruited many important Gentiles, is nothing other than a clever way of concealing Jewish crimes. Thus the Jew attempts to secure key positions among the peoples so that he can support his racial comrades, enabling them to continue unhindered their exploitation, their crimes, and their murder of Gentiles.

We see this in the Congress of Vienna, in the Treaty of Versailles, in the Geneva League of Nations, as well as in international labor unions or the Bolshevist central in Moscow. It is always the same. Together with capitalism money and usury, these organizations serve the purpose of uniting Judah across all peoples and national boundaries, and concealing their misdeeds.

*Judaism and Bolshevism*

If the Jew is at the end of his resources and, despite all his care and concealment, is in danger of being discovered, he unleashes wars and revolutions. The Jews began the First World War to destroy the anti-Jewish and anti-Semitic tsarist regime. They gave Russia over to Jewish Bolshevism, and at the same time hit the inherently anti-Semitic Prussian Germany so hard that any sign of nationalist spirit was killed and destroyed.

It is entirely clear that this war, too, is the work of Judah. The Jew Rothschild said as early as 1934 that he would do everything he could to drive the world into war against National Socialist Germany.

Since, however, the Jew is numerically a tiny percentage of humanity, he must find allies and subject peoples to carry out his inhuman aims. Since, from the human standpoint, the Jew is and must be the greatest of all criminals, he must seek such help where it is to be found—namely among the trash and scum of humanity. Each people has a certain percentage of rabble and criminality. As any organism rejects filth, so a people eliminates such elements. The Jew gathers such ethnic filth and makes of it his assault force.

The Jew is also master of lies and hypocrisy, of superstition and secret mystic rites. His crazy theories and superstitions draw in healthy people who are susceptible to such things. Any doctrine, no matter how crazy, finds its disciples and supporters, and the weak and cowardly look for ways to escape their inescapable fate through sprits and superstition. It is harder to appeal to decency, truthfulness, courage, and character than it is to appeal to cowardliness, depravity, and weakness. The Jew, as a master of hypocrisy, used that to his advantage. He invented sectarianism, Freemasonry, bourgeois mysticism, and other superstitions, to lure people after him like the Pied Piper of Hamelin. Finally, the Jew knows that he can rule and destroy only when he succeeds in building walls between humanity. The phrase "divide and conquer" comes from the Jew. He is thus the enemy of any unity, of any organized progress, of any community. Because of his Jewish blood, he must declare war on any form of order in order to be able to assert himself.

He needs chaos to conceal himself. He must destroy beauty so that his ugly Jewish face does not stand out. We find the crassest embodiment of Jewish depravity in the Soviet Union.

*The Jew as Oppressor of Humanity*

— 4 —

# OVERALL, I CALL IT BOLSHEVISM

By that, I mean and will prove that Judaism and Bolshevism were and are everywhere, and at all times, the same. Moses, the founder of the Jewish rabbi state, was the first proponent of the doctrine we today call Bolshevism. From him to Stalin, there is a single red thread that runs through all of history, and is visible everywhere Judah was at work destroying human culture, human beauty, and ethnic unity.

*1. Bolshevism from Moses to Stalin has murdered, destroyed, and ruined humanity and its culture.*

The Jewish grain-speculator Joseph reduced the Egyptian people to starvation and misery through his speculation. When they realized this, they saw the Jewish depravity and freed themselves from Jewish rule by putting the Jews in concentration camps and forcing them to work. The Jew swore revenge, incited the lowest elements, and according to the Old Testament, killed thousands and thousands of Egyptian children in one night by killing the "first born." Exodus 12:7-13 and 29-30 state that there was a bloody mark on all the buildings, and that the crazed masses, led by the Jews, killed all the "first born" of Egypt.

In the Book of Esther, we read that in one bloody night, the Jews slaughtered and destroyed 75,000 Persians. Even today, the Jew celebrates Purim to commemorate his great triumph.

During the reign of the Emperor Trajan,[8] we hear of terrible mass murders in Babylon, Cyrenia, Egypt, Cyprus, in all of the Near East and around the Aegean, where the chronicles report that many, many hundreds of thousands of people—men, women, and children—were butchered in the most gruesome ways. The children of Bethlehem may have been murdered during this period, a fate to which Christ nearly fell victim. Here, too, we hear of a disgusting Jewish deed of the worst and basest

---

[8] From 98 to 117 AD.

type. The whole Old Testament is a chronicle of Jewish robberies, mass murder, tortures, thievery, and misdeeds.

However, it is not only in the Near East or the Roman Empire that we hear of Jewish murder and Jewish bloodthirstiness. It happens wherever the Jew goes. St. Bartholomew's Night and its horrors, and the French Revolution with its guillotine, were the work of Jewish bloodthirstiness. Today, we know that the death of 4,000 people in Lower Saxony was the result of advice given by a Jew to Charlemagne. The butchering of 1½ million Northern Albigensians by Asiatic hordes is also the fault of the Jews, who even then had influence on the Roman curia.

The Crusades, with their enormous sacrifices in the blood of northern peoples, were the result of Jewish insanity.[9] This reached its crazed height in the Children's Crusade, which sent tens of thousands of German children against well-armed and well-trained Turkish soldiers.

Oliver Cromwell and the Puritans committed regicide and mass murder under the banner of the Lion of Judah, and took the Old Testament with them in their saddlebags so that they would always have the murderous commands of the Jewish tribal god Jehovah close at hand.[10]

The Inquisition and the bestial witch hunts, in which streams of Nordic blood were shed, and which had the devilish goal of destroying the Nordic race, were the work of the Jew Diego Laynez, who became the superior general of the Jesuit order.

The Thirty Years War, born from the religious insanity of Jewish thinking, killed 13 million of the 17 million German people.[11] Only four million escaped Jewish bloodthirstiness. The Thirty Years War was the prelude to the final destruction of European humanity. All the following conflicts, civil wars, and wars between peoples are the result of this Jewish mass murder, even aside from the fact that one finds the Jew everywhere in modern wars as a Freemason, an armaments manufacturer, or as international arsonist.

Our current age is the epitome of the Jewish desire for destruction. Never has Jewish Bolshevism presented itself so freely and openly to

---

[9] The Crusades were a series of religious wars in the Middle East running primarily from 1100 to 1300 AD. The ostensible goal was the recapture of Jerusalem from the Muslim Turks.

[10] Cromwell (1599-1658) was an English politician and military leader.

[11] The war ran from 1618 to 1648.

humanity as it does today. Now the Jew believes he can drop his hypo-
critical mask, thinking that the world is ready for Jewish world dominance—which is nothing other than Jewish destruction.

The Bolshevist revolutions in Russia, Hungary, Germany, Spain,
and everywhere else have destroyed and butchered more human beings
than were killed in the many thousands of years before.

*Concealing the Jews*

*2. Bolshevism from Moses to Stalin is the rule of the criminal, the mob, and the underworld.*

In the books of Moses, we read that a large "rabble" accompanied the Jewish exodus from Egypt.[12] The Old Testament itself reports that "much stolen property" went with them, and that the Egyptians were happy to be rid of the Jews and their rabble.

We hear of the same connection of the Jew with the rabble and the trash of the peoples from antiquity, the Roman Empire, and the history of every nation up to the present day.

The word 'proletarian' meant 'slave' in ancient Rome, and we hear that the slaves met with the Jews in the secret darkness of the catacombs and caves to conspire against the Roman state. Jewish historical writing— or better, historical falsification—presents the Roman emperors Nero and Caligula as beasts who slaughtered and persecuted Christians. Actually, they were anti-Semites who persecuted the Jews, not the Christians, because they saw them as a danger to the existence of the Roman Empire. Nero did not burn Rome down, as history records, but rather he let the Jewish ghetto burn down.

The Jewish affinity and attitude toward the rabble, the criminal class, and the underworld explains why the Jew Karl Marx gave life to the proletarian and Bolshevist movement. The goal was to subject national states and communities to the underworld.

In this world-conflict, we see both to the east and west the connection of the Jews to gangsters, the criminal world, and exploitation through stock exchanges and banks in England and the USA. It is the mobilization of the steppes and the Mongolian hordes to the east. Once again, the Jew is leading the mob and the criminals against European culture and the achievements of humanity.

---

[12] The "books of Moses," also called the Torah, are the first five books of the Old Testament: Genesis, Exodus, Leviticus, Numbers, and Deuteronomy.

*The Jew has always understood how to conceal himself behind the most varied masks*

*3. Bolshevism from Moses to Stalin means the destruction of peoples, civil war, and brotherly hatred.*

Isaiah 19:2-3 reads:

> I will stir up the Egyptian against Egyptian—brother will fight against brother, neighbor against neighbor, city against city, kingdom against kingdom. The Egyptians will lose heart, and I will bring their plans to nothing.

That is how it always was: Wherever the Jew enjoyed the hospitality of other peoples, collapse began. He saw his purpose and goal in life as spreading strife, suspicion, envy, and hatred among people. In the Roman

Empire, he set social groups and classes against each other. In the Thirty Years War, he set religious confessions and tribes against each other. The peoples of Europe fought each other. In the modern age, just as in the thousands of years before it, the Jew saw his goal as setting social groups and classes against each other, of inciting nations to class struggle and class hatred, thus destroying each other through civil war.

Whether in Egypt or Rome, the German tribes or today, it is always the same. "Divide and conquer, lie and agitate, to establish the conditions under which brothers will fight against and kill each other." This explains why all ruling men and leaders have been sworn enemies of the Jews, and must always be such.

Christ, one of the great men of humanity, condemned Judah with the sharpest words. He cursed and damned their devilish goals. His whole life was an anti-Semitic struggle against Judah and its methods. The Jew Paul, born Saul, also called Schaul, transformed the honest, noble, and elevated goals of the founder of the Christian religion into its very opposite, making them serve Jewish purposes. That may not dim the light of this great man of human history.[13]

After him, all the great luminaries of the spirit, of poetry and the arts, the emperors and kings, counts and popes always strove with all their might to free themselves of the Jewish vampire. The Roman Emperor Vespasian even tore down the Jewish temple in Jerusalem, along with its treasure house, taking their golden idols from the Jews. He believed that by driving them out of their land to the four corners of the world, he would break their power. But their evil drives brought the Jewish desire for destruction everywhere they went.

During the Middle Ages, the church took up the struggle against the Jews. Popes and cardinals brought cases of Jewish ritual murder to trial without mercy, and made saints of the victims of such bloody Jewish murder.

---

[13] Ley adopts the standard National Socialist line of an 'Aryan Jesus' and of a noble, 'original' Christianity. In fact, Jesus was almost certainly an ethnic Jew, a rabbi, who agitated against Roman rule and consequently got crucified. The Jew Paul and the Jewish Gospel writers virtually constructed the resurrected Jesus narrative from whole cloth; they were fraudsters and hoaxers. There was no noble, original Christian theology.

The great German Martin Luther saw through the Jew (unfortunately too late), and called for burning his synagogues and Jewish schools and covering them with earth "so that no one will ever again be able to see so much as a stone or a cinder of what remains." Speaking of what we formerly tolerated out of ignorance, Luther went on to say:

> I did not know it myself, God forgive us, but now that we know, we may not protect these places any longer. In them, they defame Christ and us, insult us, curse us, spit on us, defile us. To ignore it would be to do these things to ourselves. We must also destroy their dwellings, since there they do the same things they do in their schools. ... Some may think I say too much. I do not say too much, but rather too little, for I see what they write.

Unfortunately, Luther came to this realization only in his old age, only after he had translated the Jewish testament, with its devilish doctrines of the Jewish tribal god Jehovah, into German, thereby causing the greatest possible spread of these satanic doctrines.[14]

The same ideas are found in the writing and thinking of the great men of humanity: Schopenhauer and Goethe, Kant and Richard Wagner, up to our own day.[15]

---

[14] See Luther's book *On the Jews and their Lies* (2020; T. Dalton, ed; Clemens & Blair).

[15] For the views of these and many other eminent scholars, see Thomas Dalton, *Eternal Strangers* (2020; Castle Hill).

— 5 —

# THE JEW'S WEAPON IS MONEY, HIS IDOL IS GOLD

The methods and means of the Jew are superstition, starvation, assassination, terror, and the rule of usury; his goal is world domination; and beyond world domination, as Adolf Hitler said, the destruction of the world. We Germans learned enough about starvation as a result of the blockade during the last war. Assassination caused the First World War, and terror is the method that is supposed to force Germany to the ground in this world war. History, above all English colonial history, provides hundreds and thousands of examples of this Jewish-Puritan mentality. It is enough simply to mention these methods to recall the whole reprehensible Jewish mentality. But I do wish to say more about the world domination of gold.

The whole liberal economic order is based on gold, and the Jew has masterfully understood how to give gold an almost mystic power. Gold has had absolute power over humanity and its peoples ever since the days of the "Golden Calf" and the golden treasures of Solomon's temple in Jerusalem. The absolute dominance of gold was so strong that people no longer dared to resist it. People accepted as a god-given truth that gold was the measure of all values and of everything. But, one asks, where does this view of gold really come from? Gold has only a modest significance for human life. One could almost say that human life would continue with no difficulty if gold had never existed.

As a metal, gold is much too soft to have any practical use. It is not hard like other metals. One cannot use it to build bridges, buildings, or machines, nor to build weapons. The fact that it does not oxidize says little in terms of value, for it is surpassed in this regard by platinum. The actual ability of gold to meet human needs is zero. Despite that fact, gold has been able to dominate the world over the centuries and millennia! The value of gold is completely artificial, a pseudo-value, that can only be understood as an enormous swindle and deceit on the part of the Jew.

The dominance of gold is founded on the lies of the Jew. Gold is the Jew's weapon.

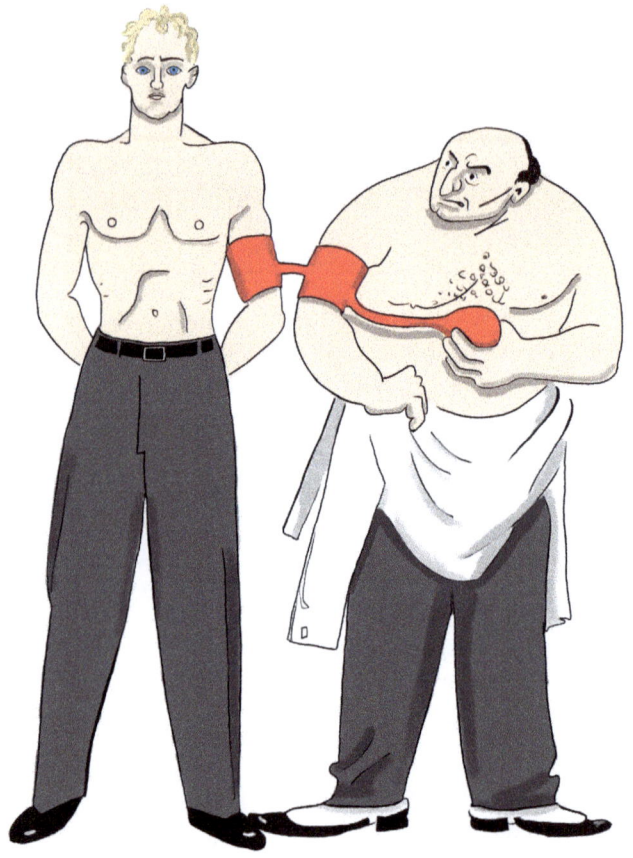

*The Jew corrupts pure-race peoples with his bad blood*

The truth of this claim by us National Socialists is shown by the fact that several Jews in the Rothschild Bank set the price of gold each day. They are the proprietors of the following banking houses:

N. M. Rothschild and Sons,
Marcus Samuel & Co.,

Samuel Montagu and Co.,
Saemy Japhet and Co.,
Mocatta & Goldsmid (official agents of the
Bank of England for gold and silver bars)

The insanity of this Jewish dealing is shown by the statement of a German economic leader to an American business friend. This American could not understand how National Socialist Germany had maintained not only a stable currency, but also built a flourishing economy out of economic chaos, all without any gold reserves. And now, it dared wage war on England and France, the guardians of gold, without any vast war chest of gold. The German industrialist, a well-known economic leader, answered the American in this way:

You Americans possess gold mines in South Africa, and employ many, many workers there, who each year mine an enormous amount of gold. After a difficult refining process, the gold is shipped to America, where it is buried once again in fireproof and theft-proof vaults, making it sort of a new kind of gold mine. Perhaps it will be rediscovered in a hundred or a thousand years, and your successors will move the gold back to Africa. Do you not see how crazy that all is? The economy of the world is founded on such nonsense.

We Germans have put an end to it since Adolf Hitler took power. We use our time and our people to do useful things, and we have proven that labor, and the production of necessary things, are a secure foundation for our economy. It is much better than your gold rush!

I have been told that the American left with a very thoughtful expression on his face.

Jewry has persuaded the peoples of the earth to accept this bluff, this swindle, and has built a whole system of lies and fraud. Their goal is to establish and defend the rule of the Jews over human beings and peoples. As long as the peoples of the earth believe in this swindle, the five Jewish bankers named above are the real lords of the Earth. All the other so-called leaders of the peoples, all the kings and emperors, all the parliaments and democracies, all the economies and classes, are only pieces on the chessboard of these gold and money lords.

Since the churches and sciences have also bowed down to this rule of gold over the years, they also are not free of Jewry and its devilish system. They all dance around the Jewish golden calf. Gold is their idol, and the meaning of their earthly life.[16]

We recently read the news that the House of Rothschild has organized a consortium of banks to finance the war supplies flowing from the United States to England and France. This was a brief announcement, easy to overlook. However, it revealed the deepest and truest meaning of this struggle:

- The battle of money against labor;
- The hatred of the Jew for National Socialism;
- The alliance between Jewry, England, the USA, and Soviet Russia to rule the peoples of the world.

This fact shows clearly how seriously Jewry takes the situation, and the prospects of this war.

---

[16] We recall the words of Marx: "What is the profane basis of Judaism? Practical need, self-interest. What is the worldly cult of the Jew? Huckstering. What is his worldly god? Money. ... Money is the jealous god of Israel, beside which no other god may exist." ("On the Jewish Question"; 1843).

# — 6 —
# MOSES ROTHSCHILD
# VERSUS THE GERMAN WORKER

Who is Rothschild? The man Rothschild has almost become a mystic concept for the world. The founder of the "House" of Rothschild was a filthy ghetto Jew from Frankfurt. There was an unfortunate era in the history of the German states: one viewed Rothschild's birthplace much as one viewed the birthplace of Goethe, the greatest German poet. The single "service" of this "great man" of Jewry was that he, with his sons, spread a devilish financial system across Europe. It trapped the peoples and their emperors and kings in their web, where it sucked them dry, like a spider.

The world's leaders used the Jews over the centuries to exploit their people with usury and interest. For the counts and bishops, the Jews were the bloodsuckers that they constantly set loose on their subjects. After the Jew had sucked himself full, these leaders periodically took it all back. Each count and lord had his court Jew, who in turn organized an army of Jewish parasites and bloodsuckers. This primitive, but very effective, system prevailed in Poland up to the beginning of the war. The German victory freed the Polish people from the satanic methods of its big businessmen and big landowners.

In Western Europe, however, the Jews were themselves in control, as a result of the ideology of the French Revolution. Soon, the counts, even the kings and emperors, even the churches, were slaves of the Jew —dependent on his money, subject to his usury. The Jew won ever-new privileges. He created modern democracy, invented parliaments, founded parties, deposed monarchs, unleashed revolutions, started wars. In short, the Jew succeeded within a century in subjecting count and people, city and country, classes and the church. They all groaned and suffered as they paid the Jew's tribute. Anyone who refused was destroyed. Even Napoleon was a victim of the Jew. Entire peoples were ruined by this Asiatic swarm of locusts, and, if necessary, devoured and destroyed. The dance around the Jewish golden calf steadily increased in tempo.

The Jew Rothschild was the greatest among the Jews, almost the king of the Jews. One spoke of the "Rothschild dynasty." Their representatives in Frankfurt, Vienna, Paris, and London had long since become nobles, barons, and lords. And, of course, depending on where they were, they became good Germans, Austrians, Frenchmen, or Englishmen. Naturally these Jewish snobs were joined by, and begat, princes and princesses, counts and countesses, for Rothschild was a "dynasty".[17]

---

[17] The original founder was Amschel Moses Rothschild (1710-1755); his son, Mayer Amschel Rothschild (1744-1812) began the financial empire.

# — 7 —
# HE WHO DINES WITH THE JEW DIES!

What we have covered is enough to briefly show the essential character-istics of the Jew—his origins, his religion, his mentality, his methods, and his world alliance. The Jew means *death*, and therefore the battle against the Jew is an unavoidable necessity for anyone who wants to live.

As far back in human history as we look, we can establish that all young, healthy, and strong peoples banned the Jews from their communi-ty, and kept away from them. The Egyptians drove the Jews through the Red Sea, the Persians persecuted them, Christ led a bitter struggle against them, the Greeks and the Romans firmly held to the purity of race, and kept the Jews from their territory as long as they were strong and powerful.

During the heights of the Medieval period, Jews were kept in ghet-tos, and the church was the bitterest opponent of the Jews. There is a proverb from those days that is truer today than ever: "He who dines with the Jew dies." Whenever peoples have been alert, they were also con-scious of their race, and did not tolerate the plague-carrying Jew among them. They always persecuted them and rooted them out (*ausgerottet*), or at least isolated them in a ghetto as evil carriers of disease.

The Jew and those dependent on him view such ages as "back-ward," and call them "dark and sinister." The Jew, and those in his pay, call them the Dark Ages, or even the darkest Middle Ages; and in the same breath, they call Jewish emancipation, and the resulting Jewish domination, "modern." The most advanced form of human life, to them, is where the Jews have absolute control, such as in Moscow and New York. It does not bother them at all that the era that they speak of as "dark" was in fact, for those peoples and humanity, actually a period of flowering, of high culture, and of great progress, whereas the century the Jew calls "modern" is characterized by the worst poverty, by terrible de-cay, and the greatest misery. As long as it goes well for the Jew, he does not worry about what happens to anyone else.

*Europe united in a battle for freedom against Bolshevism and Jewry*

Let us not be deceived by the slogans that conceal the Jews. The Jewish problem is the same today as it always was, and in fighting against Judah, we find ourselves in the best company in history. Today, as in the past and the future, the proverb is still true: "He who dines with the Jew dies!" He who tolerates the Jew, who takes on his customs, who works with him, who adopts his mentality, who eats, drinks, and lives with him, who even thinks the Jew is chosen and believes he can learn something from the Jew, who expects the salvation of the world to come from the Jews—he will inevitably be ruined by Judah. He will die from it, just as the Egyptians, Persians, Greeks, and Romans did after they grew old and could no longer defend themselves against the Jews. Judah is like a vulture that attacks its victims as they are dying. It sucks their last drop of blood, leaving them to die in misery, and then seeks a new victim. The danger is greatest when he settles down and makes himself at home. When the Jew moves in, it is a sign of age, weakness, and disease. *The Jew means death!*

On the other hand, fighting against the Jews is a sign of youth, strength, self-confidence, a will to life, and of a confidence in life. He who gets rid of the Jews becomes healthy, and enters an age of unimaginable flowering, greatness, and splendor. Over the centuries and millennia, that is the clearest and strongest teaching of history. "He who dines with the Jew dies," and he who fights the Jew, destroys him, and radically frees himself from him, lives, and will never die. We Germans must think about that, and act accordingly!

Have we really done all we can to drive the Jew and his world, his spirit and his deviltry, from our midst? Many people think that it is enough to physically remove the Jew, and that if we do not see him any longer, and if we rarely see the yellow star, the Jewish problem in Germany will be solved. They say, "What more could be done about the Jews? To do more would be to take the Jew too seriously, to fight against windmills. Our hatred of the Jews would make us ridiculous Don Quixotes. Enough is enough."

These Germans are mistaken; their opinion only proves that they understand the Jewish problem either superficially, or not at all. Is it enough to destroy the louse, but leave the brood alive? Is it enough to free *ourselves* of the pest, yet deal with others who are still infested with the pest? The brood that we leave alive is the Jewish world: the Jewish mentality, the Jewish spirit, that still surrounds us, that follows us everywhere. And we still find infested neighbors in Europe—above all among our enemies, and in particular with Bolshevism.

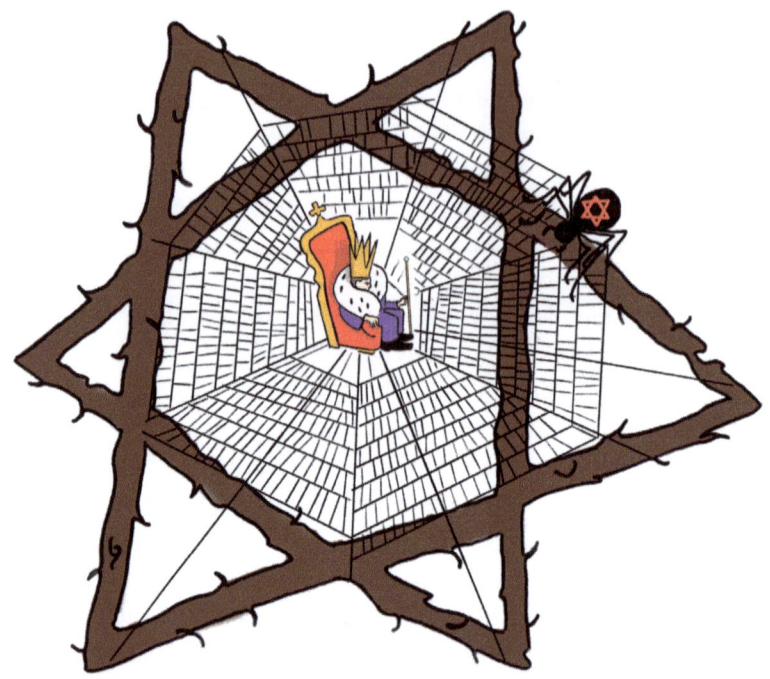

*Nobles and royal houses caught in the Jews' web*

The Jewish mentality and the Jewish spirit are the worldview of fatalism, of ghosts and spirits, of terror, of anxiety and fear, of the money bag and capitalism, of the denial of life and surrender, of begging and pity, of those who lack will, of the cowards—in a word, the bourgeois-Marxist world in which we who are older grew up. That is why it is so hard to free ourselves from it.

The Jew Paul wanted to take everything from us—God and our German soul. The nation, according to his doctrines, means nothing; it is a human stew that includes everyone from the lowest Hottentot to the best German. The Jew is "chosen" to bring us Germans "salvation." The Pauline doctrine promises heaven to those who subject themselves to it, but hell to those who reject Jewish dogma. What have we, who are not Jews, to do with Moses and the Jewish prophets? At a time when the German people is fighting for its life against Jewry, who dares to speak to us of the rabbis named Abraham, Isaac, Jacob, and all the rest of them? The Pauline doctrines call upon Jehovah, the terrible Jewish god. The "Jehovah's Witnesses" and their kin plague our air, and daily remind us that we are a long way from overcoming the Jew. The physical Jew has been removed from our midst, but his Mosaic and Pauline spirit still lives among us. Anyone who has any ties at all to it can never fight completely and radically against the Jews. Such a man's strength is weakened; he cannot use his full energies. Remember, German: "He who dines with the Jew dies." Decide! Be decisive!

*The Jew Bribes and Is Bribed*

The same is true of the capitalist world. Here, too, many Germans are dependent on the Jew and his thinking. They have contempt for the Jew, but dance around his "golden calf." These reactionaries cannot free themselves from the capitalist bonds of gold, anonymous shares of stock, interest, the lust for money, the magic of banks and stock exchanges. A man and his labor are to them, even today, merely something to be purchased, and they cannot set aside their dominating capitalism attitude. They got fat under liberalism, and are stuck in reactionary attitudes. Old men still captive to Jewish thinking are not all that great a threat, for they will die out. However, we must ensure that the young grow up under National Socialism, and are not corrupted by capitalism's poison.

Here, too, the proverb is true: "He who dines with the Jew dies." He who accepts the Jew's money and earns his money through those exploitative methods will be ruined. He who holds work in contempt, who sees his German racial comrade as those to be exploited, who sees labor as a product like herring and cotton, is an enemy of the people, a traitor, and deserves no pity.

The counterpart of this Jewish-capitalistic thinking is the twin of capitalism: the Jewish changeling and Jewish bastard, Bolshevism. Each resembles the other. I do not believe that they have many supporters in Germany.

## — 8 —
# JUDAH MUST DIE!

In this struggle against Judah, there is only a clear either/or. Any half measure leads to one's own destruction. Judah and its world must die if humanity wants to live; there is no other choice than to fight a pitiless battle against the Jews in every form, and not to give up until the last Jewish thinking has been destroyed everywhere.

Here, I wish to let the Jew Kurt Münzer speak about his race. In his first novel *The Way to Zion*, published in 1910, Münzer, rather like Walter Rathenau in his essay "Hear, O Israel," holds up a Jewish mirror to the Jews and shows them completely without masks. He writes:

> Not only we Jews are a degenerate, dried-out, used-up culture. All of the races of Europe are as well. Perhaps we have infected them? Ruined their blood? Jewified everything? Our thinking is in everything living, our spirit rules the world. We are the lords, for what has power today is our spiritual child. One may hate us, persecute us. Our enemies may triumph over our physical weakness. We can no longer be gotten rid of. We have conquered the races, defiled them, broken their power, made everything rotten, foul, and decayed with our stale culture. Our spirit is no longer to be exterminated.

The Jew Münzer was wrong in his superiority complex, since only 30 years later, the Jew has been exterminated in Germany and Europe.[18]

We National Socialists have exterminated the Jewish spirit and the Jews themselves in Germany. We will not cease this struggle until the

---

[18] By "exterminated" (*vernichtet*), Ley means not the physical killing of the Jews but rather their complete removal from the Reich, as we can see from his discussion above. And yet, as we see in the following lines, Ley is not averse to, someday, seeing "Judah" "die"—although the exact meaning of this is ambiguous. For more on the fate of the Jews under Hitler, see T. Dalton, *Debating the Holocaust* (2020, 4th ed; Castle Hill).

final judgment has been spoken against the Jews. Judah must die! Anti-Semitism will triumph throughout the world. The central Jewish newspaper, the *Jewish Chronicle*, writes: "Anti-Semitism is Germany's secret weapon, for Germany has pursued it consistently, making it a universal problem that will occupy all peoples."

That is correct. The Jew hit the target, and the Jew knows the danger. This war was started by the Jews; it is a Jewish war in its deepest roots. It will be the same as the Jewish reaction to the National Socialist uprising in 1923. The Jews believed then that their hirelings could exterminate the National Socialist movement with blatant force, murder, and prisons. They achieved the opposite. Until then, National Socialism was limited to Munich, or at most Bavaria, but afterwards it spread almost explosively throughout the entire German Reich. It was as if one had opened a sack of pollen that spread its seed into the last German town and village.

*Even the French Revolution displayed the Jewish symbol, the Star of David*

So it is today. One believes it is possible to exterminate anti-Semitism with fire and sword, phosphorus, and bombs. But they find that anti-Semitism has become a worldwide problem that occupies all peoples. What was once only a German problem has become a European, an English, even an American problem. We hear that Jews in England and the USA are already suffering under it.

When the English and Americans finally realize that they are fighting in reality for the freedom of the Jews, they will become reluctant, and will become critical of the Jews; they will truly *discover* the Jews. That is enough to make an anti-Semite of any Aryan. That is what the *Jewish Chronicle* means when it complains: "Anti-Semitism has become a universal problem." That is true! The Jew is being discovered in the entire world as a result of this war; he loses his concealment, and is thus already defeated. Anti-Semitism is "Hitler's secret weapon," which will lead us Germans to inevitable victory!

# — 9 —
# EUROPE AWAKENED

It is clear that it will take time for our part of the Earth to grow together. A civil war that has lasted a thousand years cannot be overcome in a year. Nonetheless, the increase in cooperative work between the European peoples has greatly increased in recent years. The struggle against Bolshevism will drive them even closer together. Jewish Bolshevism is at the gates, and must be fought, whatever the cost. This common defensive battle teaches peoples to appreciate each other, and the Jew on the enemy side, with his Jewish stupidity and arrogance, does the rest of what has to be done. Here we can only say: We are happy that our enemies have their Jews.

What all the eloquence on European cooperation has not achieved, the Jew in his blindness will quickly hammer into the European peoples the knowledge that they must stand together in their battle against Bolshevism and in their battle against the Anglo-barbarians, that they share a common struggle against Judah. Our allies and their brave soldiers, the European legions of the Norwegians, Danes, Dutch, Flemish, Walloons, the many millions of Europeans hard at work in Germany—all these are proof that Europe has awakened, and is beginning to find a European community in the midst of hard sacrifices and suffering, in the midst of incendiary and explosive bombs.

I remember a French legend, from a French play, that shows how Europe is building a community: Edmond Rostand brilliantly illuminates the French mentality. His comedy is set in a chicken yard, where many beautiful hens have gathered around to admire one of the finest roosters. The rooster, of course, constantly says that the sun rises only because he crows, and that the light of the world comes from his almighty crowing. One day, this proud rooster no longer crows, because of his age. He has grown old and weak, and is no longer able to crow. But the sun still rises. The vain rooster cannot survive the blow. He dies from injured vanity and wounded pride.

Charlemagne, Prince Eugene, Frederick the Great, Napoleon Bonaparte, and Victor Hugo all wanted a united Europe, and fought for it. As

Napoleon Bonaparte sat in St. Helena, miserable and demoralized, he wrote the following prophetic words: "I failed. I was not strong enough to unify Europe. But someone will come after me who will raise my banner once more, and finish my work, and then no one will speak of England any longer, but rather one will speak of a Napoleon."

These prophetic words of Napoleon Bonaparte, England's sworn enemy, are now being fulfilled. European unity is being forged now that the Jew has been driven from it. Under the leadership of its Führer Adolf Hitler, Germany will carry the banner of this ancient, yet ever-young, part of the Earth. At the end of this war, Germany will win and Europe will be united!

# BOOK TWO

---

## "The Jew as World-Parasite"

by
Hans-Georg Otto

*A Plague on the World*

# INTRODUCTION

*The Jew wins with the lie
and dies with the truth.*
—Adolf Hitler

In this war, which is about the existence or non-existence of the German people, we must remind ourselves daily that it was the Jews that unleashed this war against us. It makes no difference whether he confronts us as a Bolshevik or a plutocrat, as a Freemason or in some other guise, or even without any mask at all; the Jew always remains the same. He is the one who has incited and swayed the assorted peoples who stand against us today, so that they have become, in effect, the obedient tools of international Jewry.

The way the Jew has utilized large groups of peoples and states against us has already been demonstrated in two previous booklets, "*Battle of Destiny in the East*" and "*Europe and America.*" Both are the intellectual precursors of this booklet. Explicitly at the beginning of the sixth year of the war, we must not allow ourselves to mistake the Jewish Question in any way.[1] That is why we must, first of all, always work against the many lingering remnants of earlier educational influences and the generally common view, according to which Judaism is to be regarded as merely a religious denomination. In fact, it is rather the Judaic racial mixture that must be emphasized. The question of the particular religious beliefs of the Jews, therefore, should be completely ignored, and instead we must focus solely on its human racial foundations.

From the very beginning of its existence, the National Socialist German Worker's Party (NSDAP) has repeatedly worked to enlighten the German people about the basic facts. As early as 1922, the Führer said:

> We were the ones who, for the first time, pointed out to the people that a danger was creeping in on us, which millions

---

[1] The "sixth year" refers to the sixth calendar year: 1939 to, here, 1944.

of Germans no longer recognized and which will lead us all to our downfall, the danger of the Jews.

Or in his book *Mein Kampf,* where he says:

> [The Jew] can live among other peoples only as long as he succeeds in persuading them that he himself is not a race but a 'religious community'—though of a special sort.[2]

This first and greatest lie, that the Jewish Question is not a racial matter, but is instead a religious one, is then inevitably followed by further lies.

This includes another lie about how the Jew uses language. For the Jew, language is not the means by which he expresses his thoughts, but the means by which he *conceals* them. In speaking, for example, German, French, or any other language, he still thinks in a Jewish manner. And while he may spout German verse, he is only living out the essence of his race. The best-known example of this is Heinrich Heine.[3]

How important such comprehensive educational reform is, which, even before the existence of the NSDAP was being carried out by some decent Germans, we can best recognize by looking at the recent history of our people. In past generations, it was still considered vulgar to raise the Jewish Question. People deliberately closed their minds to all these issues, even if the individual Jew in question was instinctively perceived as an alien.

Why nonetheless do we Germans, and almost we alone, fight Judaism so vigorously? Why do we repeatedly find times in our German history when the German element in particular turns against Judaism? Alfred Rosenberg, in his book *The Track of the Jew Through the Ages,* provides the answer to this question:

> There is probably no other nation in Europe that has pursued and explained the inner mechanisms of humanity as much as the German. Therefore, the German comprises, in its deepest essence, the spiritual antipode of the Jews…

---

[2] *Mein Kampf,* vol. 1, sec. 11.12, p. 307 (2022, Clemens & Blair edition).
[3] Heine (1797-1856) was a prominent Jewish-German poet and writer.

Despite all this, the power of Judaism and its supporters had become so great among the German people that it led to the collapse of 1918.[4] The reason for this lies primarily in the fact that, in connection with the tremendous numerical growth of our people and the liberal currents that set in at the same time, more and more Germans failed to recognize the naked truth of the racial problem and thus became indifferent to the danger of the Jews.

In recent years, the National Socialist worldview has opened the eyes of the greater part of our race to this problem. The Germans have discovered that, like a parasite, the Jew has wormed his way in, not only into the lives of our people, but into all the peoples of the world. And by internally hollowing out the primal racial strength of the peoples, he wants to destroy their ethnic and national existence, and then become master over them.

It is wrong, however, for some Germans to conclude from the fact that since the Jew has been eliminated from German politics, that Jewish influence has also been entirely eliminated from our thoughts and actions. Here and there, people even express the superficial opinion that this is also the case with other races of the world, to the extent that they have followed our example. But this is now only the case for a few. Rather, we must remember that, according to conservative estimates, there are around 16 million religious Jews living around the world, and that a good 10 million of them (over 60%) live in Europe alone, and 4.5 million (about 30%) live in America; and then 800,000 in Asia, 530,000 in Africa, and 25,000 in Australia. This summary of the figures alone makes it clear why the Jewish danger threatens Europe uniquely to an extraordinary degree. But we understand that the rapid growth of Judaism in America represents a particular danger for us as well. Right now, the Jew is shifting his main forces to the Western Hemisphere, in order to be able, as he believes, to wage war against us from there in a secure position.

Despite the fact that he feels so safe for the moment, the Jew is thinking a great deal about why the awakened peoples of Europe have take up such a strong defensive position against him. Nothing characterizes his uncertainty on the path to world domination, mandated to him by

---

[4] That is, the November Revolution of 1918, when activist Jews within Germany led a popular uprising that ousted the Kaiser and led to Germany's defeat in World War One.

his holy law, more than the considerations of the kind we often find in Jewish writers.

It is partly this uncertainty that forces the Jew to want to achieve his goals of world supremacy even faster and more viciously. As Goethe said in his day: "The Jew will not spare us." We can be sure today that the Jew remains true to this principle more than ever. In the book *Now and Forever* by Samuel Roth, it is revealed how the Jewish world-parasite imagines the realization of his final goal: the achievement of world domination. With all the fervor of faith available to Judaism, it depicts the appearance of the avenger who wanders from country to country, gathering his horde, at the head of which, he obliterates Europe with sadistic cruelty and a lust for destruction—a Europe that would not bow to the Jew and opposed his path to world supremacy.

We National Socialists believe the Führer when he says that at the end of this battle, unleashed by the Jewish world-parasite against us as its strongest opponent, Judaism will be destroyed in Europe. Until this destruction is accomplished, we must always remember that the Jew is our absolute enemy, who will stop at nothing and knows only one goal: our complete annihilation.

# — 1 —
# THE NATURE OF PARASITES

### 1. What is a parasite?

The word parasite come to us from the Greek, and translates into German as '*Mit-esser*' ("one who eats with another") or, generally speaking, a freeloader, leech, or scrounger. We first encounter the term 'parasite' in regard to nature. Ottokar Lorenz writes:

> In the economy of nature, almost all plants draw their strength from the nutrients of the soil, which they convert through their efforts into the elements of their own life and growth and organic structure. Alongside and inside we also find *parasites*. They suck out the life-juices that have already been created through the work of other plants. Their very condition for living is therefore the destruction of foreign plants, from whose absorption they live and from whose progressive destruction they themselves develop into ever greater profusion, until the death of their host—which, of course, robs them of their own basis for life.[5]

Dr. Rosenberg adds this:

> The conflict of the German genius with the Jewish demon has been unwittingly described by a half-Jew, Arno Schicke-danz, in its essential features. [In his book *Social Parasitism in the Life of Peoples*], he describes how the sack crab bores through the posterior of the pocket crab, gradually growing into the latter, sucking out its last life-strength.[6]

Modern research has identified parasites and freeloaders in nature that can only survive at the expense of their fellow creatures. Research has

---

[5] "Wirtschaft und Rasse" (*NS-Monatshefte* 19, p. 107)
[6] *Myth of the 20th Century* (2021, pp. 274-275; Clemens & Blair edition).

also shown us how animals have developed over very long processes from independent creatures into parasites that are only able to exist with a foreign host. Another example is the sheep ked (*Melophagus ovinus*), a parasitic fly that can only survive by burrowing into the skin of a sheep and feeding on its blood.

Humans have always had an instinctive abhorrence to parasitic phenomena in nature. We can see this in the general aversion to hyenas, jackals, vultures, and other similar animals, although these do not even technically meet the prerequisites of a true parasite.

Nature is in a constant battle with parasites. Plants and animals defend themselves against the invasion of these foreign bodies with all the means at their disposal. The human body too is constantly producing protective antibodies. It is a question of the biological strength of the individual human being, whether these antibodies are available to him in sufficient numbers. Today, science has come to the aid of both nature in general and humans in particular, through the invention of artificial antibodies.

The peculiarity of the earlier bourgeois way of thinking meant that people were very proud of the scientific discovery of the nature of parasites and the invention of certain defensive substances based upon it. Unfortunately, they were disinclined to extend these scientific conclusions to the life of mankind.

### 2. The Jew is the parasite of humanity

When the NSDAP, from the beginning of its struggle, repeatedly—and especially through the words of the Führer—pointed out that the Jew is a parasite, the initial response, especially among the so-called educated class, was scorn and ridicule. When the Führer pointed out that all decent humanity today suffers under Jewish parasitism, this was rejected. At best, people smiled at such a "zealot." People often knew this or that from their own bitter experience about the business practices of individual Jews, but since Judaism disguised itself as a religious community, many people, due to their own denominational views, could not muster the inner consistency to acknowledge the true nature of this purported religious community.

When the Führer went on to say:

> The man who thinks that he can bind himself by treaty with
> parasites is like a tree that believes it can form a profitable
> agreement with mistletoe.[7]

this statement was perceived as unpleasant. People had already entered
into too many ties with Judaism to be able to free themselves from them.
The Jews were more or less allowed to do as they pleased, as the Führer
said in the same passage:

> [The Jew] goes his own way—the way of sneaking in
> among nations and boring within. And he fights with his
> own weapons—lies and slander, poison and corruption, in-
> tensifying his struggle to the point of bloodily rooting out
> his hated opponents.

It is still important today to draw the Jew out from his anonymous concealment, and to be able to recognize him correctly as the world-parasite.

We therefore note: *The Jew is the parasite of humanity*. He can af-
fect individuals as a solitary parasite, entire nations as a social parasite,
and humanity as a global parasite. In order to be able to identify him in
his full form, we have to deal with his nature, which means examining
his character in detail, his views on the value of life, his claim to world
domination, and his capacity for assimilation.

---

[7] *Mein Kampf*, vol. 2, sec. 14.12, p. 292. Mistletoe is a parasitic vine that can
strangle its host tree.

# — 2 —
# THE NATURE OF THE JEW

## IIa. The Racial Origins of the Jews

### 3. Jewry: An anti-race

If we examine the racial composition of the Jews in detail, we come to the conclusion that Judaism is not a race in the common sense of the word, but must be regarded instead as an anti-race, as described by Houston Stewart Chamberlain, though the concept 'anti-race' admittedly cannot be understood as a biological term. Judaism, from a biological standpoint, represents a mixture of disparate races and racial debris that has become stable through inbreeding. The term 'anti-race,' therefore, primarily refers to the disruptive and destructive effects of Jewry on the naturally-evolved races. The exceptional position of Judaism within the human races lies, on the one hand, in the nature of the racial composition of the Jews, who have been dispersed for thousands of years, and on the other hand, in the rigid adherence of Jews to their so-called religious laws, which are based on the most blatant materialism.

Judaism emerged from a mixture of all possible races. It represents the most comprehensive racial mishmash in world history. This racial jumble is so dangerous for all peoples because it is primarily composed of the dregs of the various races that have been absorbed. The negative qualities of these races have been passed down and concentrated through many generations in Judaism. From this artificial, rootless racial mixture, based solely on the most blatant materialism, the parasitic anti-race has emerged among the peoples.

The nucleus of Judaism is composed of the confluence of various rootless, outcast, antisocial, sick, and degenerate elements from different races, predominantly of Near-Eastern and Oriental origin. It should be remembered here that in antiquity, lepers, for example, were expelled from their racial community, as were criminal and other misanthropic elements.

## 4. The Jewish racial mixture is constantly supplemented by anti-social elements

Due to its dispersal among the peoples for several thousand years, Judaism has parasitically infested almost all the races on Earth. As a social parasite, it affects first and foremost the lowest classes of people—the slaves, the proletarians, the rabble, and so on, as they offer the least resistance to the Jewish parasite. These sections of the population, most of whom have lost their natural instinct against racial aliens, constitute the point of entry of Jewish blood.

Already in the Old Testament (Exodus 12:38) we read about the departure of the children of Israel from Egypt: "And a lot of rabble went with them."

Since these under classes were already strongly inclined toward criminality and antisocial behavior, and had a tendency toward political upheaval, the Jewish racial mixture absorbed into itself the negative characteristics of these races and increased them from generation to generation, passing them on and strengthening them. By interbreeding with the lowest layers of other races, the Jewish anti-race became more and more perfected toward the negative side. This artificial mishmash of races was kept together by the compulsion of a materialistic, so-called religious law, geared toward this world, which promised its followers a comfortable life on Earth and dominion over all the peoples and nations. This Jewish racial mixture was kept away from the influence of foreign deities with the utmost severity.

During the Babylonian captivity, which lasted for several hundred years, the coalescence of this Jewish racial mishmash was promoted through inbreeding.[8] From this point on, the absorption of foreign elements was largely prohibited, so that we encounter the Jewish anti-race for the first time in history as a fairly clearly-defined and demarcated, internally stable type.

With increasing numerical strength, Judaism isolated itself more and more from the outside world and formed a state within a state. In general, mixing blood with other peoples only occurred and was permit-

---

[8] The Babylonian captivity ran from 597 to 538 BC, hence about 60 years. But if we consider the precursors and aftermath, the effects extended over centuries.

ted by the rabbis if it entailed an economic or political advantage for the individual Jew and for the local Jewish community.

As inherent in its genetic material, this Jewish anti-race has sustained the bad qualities of all races throughout the centuries, and through negative selection has perfected them to the highest degree. The Jewish racial mixture predominantly bears the traits of the Near Eastern and Oriental races, but traces of the Eastern, Western, and Nordic races can also be detected. In many cases, Mongolian and Negroid traits appear as well.

### 5. The main groups in the Jewish racial mixture

Even the "Jewish Lexicon" cannot avoid identifying eight different main groups that were decisively involved in the development of Judaism, and in this way must affirm that it arose from an unholy racial conglomeration. But modern research also distinguishes the following groups and components:

1) The Patriarchs, who came from southern Babylon and migrated via northern Babylonia to Canaan (around 2200 BC);

2) The Hittites, who intermarried with the Patriarchs in Canaan;

3) The Canaanites, a mixed population of Arab Semites with later Babylonian, Egyptian, and Hittite components, which immigrated through colonization and foreign rule. They were gradually absorbed by the invading tribes of Judah and Israel through military operations (enslavement, proselytism to prisoners of war, and intermarriage with female slaves), later through peaceful assimilation and intermarriage (1000 to 800 BC);

4) The large group of people from the time of the "Egyptian bondage" (around 1200 BC), who, through legitimate intermarriage and the acquisition and conversion of slaves, documented in numerous passages in the Bible, the Jews acquired Arab as well as Negroid racial elements. Furthermore:

5) Indo-European elements, through several hundred years of mixing, first as slaves, then through assimilation with the Philistines, who were probably of Nordic origin (900 to 400 BC);

6) Greeks and Romans, through intermarriage and the assimilation of slaves in the centuries of Hellenism and Roman rule in Judea (300 to 70 BC);

7) Proselytes from a variety of peoples in the centuries of the collapse of the ancient world, the conversion of pagans, and the abolition of slavery (from 1 to 1000 AD), such as Arabs, Egyptians, Babylonians, Syrians, Persians, Armenians, Greeks, Romans, Mauritanians, Celts, Slavs, Hungarians, etc.

Thus, it can be seen that Judaism, from a racial point of view, is a phenomenon that has emerged from the races—mixed races and racial debris of many peoples. After its amalgamation, it was held together only by its rigid materialistic religious laws and the prohibition of mixing with members of foreign peoples.

## 6. The Ashkenazim and the Sephardim

When we discuss the racial origins of the Jews, we must also include an explanation of the emergence of the Ashkenazim and the Sephardim. After the Roman destruction of Jerusalem [in 70 AD], the diaspora of the Jews resulted in their division into two main groups, one of which spread across Turkey, the Balkans, Hungary, northern Italy, Germany, Austria, Galicia, Poland, as well as southern and western Russia, while the other covered the region coinciding with the greater Arabian culture, North Africa and the Mediterranean countries as far as Spain.

As a result of moving into vastly different ethnic and cultural spheres, as well as inhabiting very different climate conditions, they developed over time into two different types: the Eastern-type or Ashkenazi Jew, and the Spanish-type or Sephardic Jew. In the former we find a stronger influence of Slavic and Turanian (Turkic) blood, while in the Sephardim we find a greater influence of the Mediterranean race.

## 7. Non-Jewish proselytes in the Jewish religious community

In addition to the group of people who belong to Judaism in racial terms, there are also some non-Jewish ethnic splinter groups who call themselves Jews because they have adopted the Jewish faith, but have nothing to do with Judaism in racial terms. Examples of such ethnic grafts on the Jewish faith are:

- the Yemenite Jews of Arabia, who converted to Judaism around 450 AD;
- the Falash Mura in Ethiopia;
- the Mountain or Caucasus Jews near the Caspian Sea;
- the Georgian Jews (Grusinian), tribes from the Iranian race, who later merged with the Kyrgyz (Mongols of the Volga plain) and were probably converted to Judaism by Jews from Persia;
- the black Jews of Bombay, Hindustanis, who were probably converted by Spanish Jews;
- the Kaifeng Jews in the Chinese province of Henen;
- the Marambu Jews of the Angolan Loango coast, who live according to Jewish ritual;
- and the Khazars.

These foreign tribes, which were introduced to Judaism through proselytism—that is, through religious conversion—belong to the Jewish religious community today, but were not brought into the racial mixture and are not part of Judaism in the narrower sense. This fact also corroborates Judaism's adherence to strict racial isolation.

## 8. Judaism and inbreeding

This brief overview of the racial ancestry of the Jews shows us the uniqueness of the origins and composition of Jewry, which is in stark contrast to the origins and development of all other races. Judaism, as we have seen, has not, like other races, grown organically on a certain foundation in the course of a national history, in contact and conflict with other peoples, through trade and war. Nor has it tried, like other races, to expand its population through diligence and hard work.

Judaism is neither a race nor a mixed race. It is an inextricable jumble of races, racial mixtures, and racial debris, artificially held together by its rabbis. Effectively, it is a kind of anti-race, that can only have a destructive effect, not a constructive one. Judaism is the artificial union of a variety of antisocial, criminal, diseased, degenerate, and outcast elements from all the possible races of the world of classical antiquity, brought together through inbreeding.

In our sense, Judaism is neither a race, nor a people, nor a religion. Nor does it have a homeland, but leads a rootless parasitic existence at the expense of its host peoples. Its homeland today is primarily the criminal quarters of the major international cities; its god is money; and its agenda is revolutionary upheaval, the destruction and annihilation of the cultural assets of mankind.

## IIb. Physical Appearance

### 9. Outer aspect conceals reality

Every nation that has retained its racial instinct to some extent will automatically recognize the Jew by his nature, behavior, and especially by his physical appearance. The almost universal way to recognizing the Jew in Germany was probably through the famous figures of the rural cattle Jew, the rag-and-bone man, and the crooked banker. For a long time, the representations of the physiognomy of these Jews that had become second nature to us were regarded as the typical manifestations.

The Eastern Jews, in particular, underwent their first evolutionary adaptation to European circumstances before our very eyes. They crossed the border in long caftans with ringlet curls on their cheeks and a black cap on their head. They went about their business in this clothing at first, and then slowly developed into what they called "Europeans". But even in this first stage of their assimilation, their appearance remained rather foreign to us. They had those slightly bent legs, they mumbled, they always gave the impression of being unwashed, and they smelled of garlic or musk. They announced the beginning of their social advancement with excessive ostentation by extravagantly adorning their wives, and also themselves, with all kinds of jewelry. Most of the powerful Jews of the period of German decline were able to hold on to their quickly-elevated positions only if they adopted as early as possible as much of the sheen of the greater leading world they so longed for, at least outwardly. How often have we mocked the fact that the Jews with the glossiest exteriors had not yet absorbed the contents.

Many Germans may still ask themselves today why the fight against Judaism was such a difficult and strenuous task, when there were also quite a few Jews who had emerged from these initial stages of Jewish development and had achieved a certain level of virtuosity in concealing their absolute physical deficiency. They tried to overcome their physical defects and racial peculiarities by choosing clothing and conforming behavior, and thus becoming even more dangerous to us. Now, the harmless citizen said that such a "decent Jew," whose appearance was so well-groomed, who even knew how to dress and behave elegantly, was a perfectly passable fellow. And the higher the tailor's art advanced, the more often this superficial point of view, which is so dangerous for us, was taken.

In this elective mimicry, Judaism used uncommon means of deception. One of these was the production of certain types of Jews as athletes. There were already some Jews among the sports greats of the past decades. We still remember the "Bar Kokhba" sports clubs from the period of decline. The Jews attached great importance to the fact that only those Jews whose physical appearance could keep up with the average of their host people appeared as competitors in these clubs. The apolitical world of the time was also quite captivated by this.

Indeed, the fact that the great majority of Jews, at least in their physical appearance, had not changed at all, became clear to any German that wanted to see it, when he looked at them after 1933 with a politically-trained eye. Those who were able to look into the concentration camps and labor camps were instructed in particular.

What a difference in behavior and comportment compared to us: If a German must live in a camp for a long time, perhaps even as a prisoner of war, and in more primitive circumstances than he is used to living, he will not, as a member of the Germanic race, abandon a certain dignity in behavior and manner. In particular, he will not lose the feeling for the need to maintain physical and mental freshness and purity.

## 10. Aggravating pressures

With the Jew, it's the other way around. As a parasite, and with the help of deception, as long as he strives for full equality with his host people (in order to deceive about his striving for absolute rule), he is able to bear the obligations of behavior that arise for him, contrary to his own feelings, only with the utmost effort of will. The very moment when, for general reasons, this compulsion ceases to exist, the Jew, who has perhaps presented himself as highly cultivated for decades, immediately sinks back into the dirt, into an indifference to personal hygiene and physical deportment that seems uncanny to us—and often, after just a few days.

Of course, after a few weeks, he reflects the primeval appearance of his race again: the devious, diminutive, dirty, and greasy Jew. It was a façade that he had appropriated. He was unable to change his own substance in the preceding decades—nor did he want to. If a Jew is honest, he never really cares to embrace anything from his hosts. He is firmly convinced that, in the end, he will be the master of his host peoples, and then he will be able to impose *his* law on them, by force.

## 11. Undervaluation of physical labor

One particular characteristic of Judaism is expressed in the undervaluation of physical labor. Even in terms of physical appearance, Jews were not predestined for work in the manual sense. As a result of inbreeding and their inherent racial mixture, they have elevated this to a purpose. He preferred to trade, leaving the physical labor to others. The teachings of the Talmud came to his aid. Thus in Germany we hardly ever see a Jew among the miners, the peasantry, the stone and earth workers, and similar professions involving heavy labor.

But wherever a Jew worked, there was certainly the expectation of "big business." Then, admittedly, he could put in the effort for quite some time. But what is crucial is that the Jew does not have the same ethical relationship to work that we do. For him, work is one of the various possibilities for exploitation. Not creating value, but *collecting* value —that is the Jewish goal.

## IIc. Spiritual Appearance

## 12. The conflict between German genius and the Jewish demon

We Germans have in our language the old notion of the "high-spirited man." We imagine such a person to be a figure who, equipped with the best forces of character and will, and guided by high ideals, does everything for the benefit of the whole collective. Regarding the Jew, Alfred Rosenberg writes in *The Myth of the 20ᵗʰ Century*:

> The strength of Nordic spiritual flight has been crippled. The creature of Ahasuerus,[9] earthen-heavy, sucks at the lamed muscles. Where any kind of wound is torn open in the body of a nation, the Jewish demon always eats itself into the infected part and, as a parasite, it exploits the weak hours of the great nations of this world. His mentality is not to fight as a hero for enlightened, constructive rule, but to make the world liable to financial interest. This is the direction of this parasite, strong of strong—not to fight but to creep; not to serve values, but to devaluate. These things constitute his law, according to which he has moved and from which he can never escape, as long as he exists.[10]

We stand today in this great, perhaps final confrontation between two worlds. Perhaps unconsciously, Schickedanz has characterized this conflict as one between German genius and the Jewish demon. He writes:

> The evil demon of Jewry is...Phariseeism. It is certainly the bearer of the hope of the Messiah, but simultaneously is the guardian that prevents any Messiah from arriving... That is the specific, most dangerous form of Jewish denial of the world... The Pharisee actively denies the world. He ensures that, where possible, nothing takes shape, and in so doing he is driven by a demonic emotion. This apparent denial is thus actually a particularly violent kind of world affirmation, but with negative symptoms.
>
> The Buddhist would be happy if, around him, the world fell asleep. The Pharisee would be finished if, around him, life did not wish to take on shape again and again, for then his life-function of denial would no longer find a use... They are the spirit that always denies, and with an ecstatic

---

[9] Originally, the fictional Persian king in the Book of Esther. Later, Ahasuerus became the name of the mythical wandering Jew, a curse upon the land.
[10] *Myth*, p. 274.

affirmation of a utopian existence that can never be, conceal the arrival of the Messiah. They would have to hang themselves like Judas, if the latter really came, since they are completely incapable of yes-saying.[11]

## 13. The Jew corrupts the intellectual products of his host people

Virtually nothing must be added to these words. But further clarifications of the spiritual manifestation of Judaism are as follows.

Jews were accustomed over the centuries to handing down the Talmudic teachings by memorization, and to imagining the pros and cons of their own laws in large religious meetings, finding loopholes to circumvent the laws. In order to be able to fulfill certain points of these laws particularly well, Jews have acquired a flexibility of mind during this time—something which often makes a strong impression on the unbiased observer.

Our ancestors in particular were often unable to resist being impressed by the Jewish spirit. The Jews seemed not only to understand every intellectual impulse of the Germans and the other peoples of the world, but also how to make masterful use of them. A German, for example, might have a vague thought, but a Jew gave form to it. The great Germans or other thinkers of this world may have come to some bold conclusions, but the Jew sought to be the most artful explainer of these ideas. It was overlooked, how Judaism painstakingly tried to follow the individual thought-processes of the European peoples. When it was noticed, unpolitical people marveled at how spiritually kindred Judaism seemed to be in order to be able to clarify so well the innermost motives of intellectual matters.

We people of today must recognize that the Jew was not interested in somehow vying with the great epiphanies and personalities of our world of thought. The intellectual work he put in was nothing other than a political tool for penetrating himself into the very essence of the people, inside which he intends to live and dominate henceforth. That he could use this lever for their spiritual destruction is all the better.

---

[11] *Social Parasitism in the Life of Peoples* (1927).

Spinoza is a prime example. How he used of the ideas of Descartes and Giordano Bruno, in order to claim them for himself in a form that completely changes their original meaning. This is what have they done: they pretended to be the first to really articulate these ideas, and yet they are the biggest fakers. Let us remember the way Karl Marx falsified, as the appropriate natural order of life, the German concept of genuine socialism, which is rooted in our Germanic racial inheritance, with his phantom of the dictatorship of the proletariat. This doctrine bore so deeply the traits of its Jewish inventor that the world knew only to affix his name to it: hence, "Marxism."

## 14. The "greatest" Jews are the greatest destroyers

How have the people allowed themselves to be bedazzled by the intellectual phenomenon of the Jews, and how much still today do they allow themselves to be bedazzled? What a fuss was made in Germany about the abilities of Jewish attorneys. We need only think of "the celebrated defender Dr. Max Alsberg." What praise there was for the "famous" scientist Einstein, "the Newton of our day," and for the "great" doctors Freud and Hirschfeld. How much fame was heaped up on the many Jewish university professors, and on the so-called "intellectual world" in general.

Just looking at the influence of Jews or Judaism in German literature provides the opportunity to demonstrate this, citing just a few generally less well-known examples, such as Maximilian Harden, Arthur Schnitzler, or Emil Ludwig. It is precisely here that we see that the highly vaunted Jewish intellectualism is nothing other than the bitterest and most embarrassing expression of Jewish efforts to degrade and decompose their host people.

## 15. The absence of a concept of honor

It is precisely in this context that it must be pointed out that the absence of a concept of honor in the Jewish intellectual realm is also strangely noticeable. Alfred Rosenberg comments:

> The fact that the real content of the concept of honor is remote, draws with it a swindle which is often a command-

ment of religious law. Such is laid down in the Talmud and in the *Shulchan Aruch* in a monumentally honest way. That brutal searcher for truth, Schopenhauer, called the Jews the "great masters of lies".[12]

Further, according to Kant, they are "a nation of shopkeepers and swindlers".[13] In the same context, Rosenberg once again emphatically points out that Judaism is not given to a great vision of life in the form that we are accustomed to. There can, therefore, be no question of morality in the European sense.

Starting with nauseating self-praise—"Like the lamb, so are the Jews perfectly holy" (Shir hash-shirum suta 6,6)—the books of the Talmud contain a wealth of teachings that can give us an idea of how the Jew thinks about non-Jews:

- The Jew is your comrade, the non-Jew is not your comrade. (Sanhedrin 72b, Tosafot.)
- As long as the Jews fulfill the will of Yahweh, their work will be done by the hands of others. (Berakhot 35b7.)
- It is permissible to engage the wicked of this world (the non-Jews) in a war. (Berakhot 7b15.)
- Kill the best of the non-Jews! (Tractate Soferim 15,10; Midrash Tanchuma, Beschalach 8,1)
- The belongings of the non-Jews are like the desert, whoever takes possession of them first acquires them. (Talmud tractate Bava Batra 54b2.)
- There is no marriage among the non-Jews. (Sanhedrin 74b.)

These few excerpts already give a basic idea of their so-called morality; many, even more-offensive, examples can be given. But here we refer the reader to the relevant writings of Alfred Rosenberg and Dr. Johann Pohl.

We can close this reflection with the Führer's words, which he spoke on 12 April 1922 in his speech "The Agitators of Truth." He specifically characterized the nature of Judaism:

---

[12] *Myth*, p. 427.
[13] For details on Kant's and many others' critiques, see T. Dalton, *Eternal Strangers* (2020; Castle Hill).

In this community of European cultural nations, Jewish world-Bolshevism is an absolute contaminant. It does not make the slightest contribution to our economy or our culture, but only causes confusion. It cannot come up with a single positive achievement at an international show of European and world life, but only propagandistic tables of lying numbers and inflammatory posters.

## IId. The Law of Judaism

### 16. The Talmud

The nature of the Jews, as it has been characterized in brief sketches so far, cannot be fully understood if one does not deal with *the law* of Judaism. Jews claim that their law, their Torah, is their "portable fatherland" (Heinrich Heine). Such a sweeping political statement marks at the same time the metaphysical value that Judaism attaches to its law, materialistic or idealistic. Regarding the impact of this law, Rosenberg says:

> The rabbinic Talmud has created a common outlook and a blood of unbelievable tenacity. The character of the Jews in their intermediary activity and decomposition of non-Jews has remained eternally constant, from Joseph in Egypt to Rothschild and Rathenau; from Philo, by way of David ben Solomon, up to Heinrich Heine.
>
> Until 1800, an unscrupulous moral code held first place for the training and breeding of the Jewish type. Without the Talmud and the *Shulchan Aruch*, Jewry is not conceivable as a totality.[14]

So when we speak of the law of Judaism, in addition to the Talmud and the *Shulchan Aruch* as logical expressions of the essence of Judaism, we must always include the law of the blood, according to which Jews come

---

[14] *Myth*, p. 276.

into being. One idea inherent in Jewish law, already described by Dosto-evsky, is the notion of "excrescence" or abnormal growth.

One of the best Talmud experts in Germany, Dr. Johann Pohl, has characterized the Jewish legal code of the Talmud according to its form and content in several writings. He gives a brief outline of its development and structure:

> The basis of the Talmud is to be found in the Mosaic laws laid down in the Torah. These are essentially the five books of Moses in the Old Testament, which, according to tradition, Moses wrote through the supernatural dictation of Yahweh in the 12th century BC. In a broader sense, the law is comprised of the written and oral teachings, which were set down in writing in the Torah and the Talmud and in other predecessors and continuations of the religious law, which are still valid today. The Talmud itself is divided into the Mishnah ("study by repetition"—the written collection of oral traditions) and the Gemara ("to complete"—rabbinical commentaries on the Mishnah).
>
> The Mishnah is divided into six orders, which, generally speaking, encompass the laws related to agriculture, festivals, marriage and family issues, civil and criminal matters, holy things, and the laws of purity. The six orders are further divided into 63 Tractates.[15]

## 17. *Shulchan Aruch*

Given Jews' reluctance, as was their custom, to publish the complete Talmud, and the fact that earlier partial translations were not acceptable, even to the sovereigns and the church governments of the various individual host countries, the necessity inevitably arose of compiling the varied questions of the Talmud in a kind of codex for use as a manual by Jews. After several attempts, Joseph Karo (1488-1575) wrote his codex of Jewish law in 1564/5 in Venice. Karo gave his manual the name "Shulchan Aruch," which means "Set Table." This is one of the many

---

[15] See the essay by Dr. Pohl in the *NS-Monatshefte* 1939, pp. 226-227.

attempts to put Talmudic religious law into a workable concrete form. It has prevailed and remains the authoritative manual to this day. It has been repeatedly recognized by the various Jewish organizations and is held in high regard as a general document of Jewish life.[16]

So what does the Talmud in its various Tractates, and the *Shulchan Aruch*, say? Jewish law establishes once and for all that the Jews are the chosen people, and that the Jews are, and should be, the rulers of this world, even if the general circumstances do not yet make this clear. It is only because of the Jew that the universe exists at all. Since Yahweh, the Jewish god, promised all this to the Jews, his chosen people, he requires them to be conscious at all times of the fact that they are a holy community.

Yahweh places all non-Jews into the hands of the Jews. The law preaches hatred and contempt for the non-Jew. The Jew is permitted to despise, disgrace, defile, and kill the non-Jews—all in the spirit of Yahweh, the avenging God. The Jew may debase the blood of the non-Jews—he does it in praise of Yahweh. Judaism requires that one is always aware of the task Yahweh has given, to rule over the whole world.

The Jew should therefore be a troublemaker and a warmonger, he should form a state within a state, he should strive to make non-Jewish life more Jewish, but above all he should remain a Jew. Murder, theft, lying, usury, deliberate deception, bribery, and smuggling are permitted to him, if only he persists in maintaining his own racial purity.

## 18. Jewish religious law serves to preserve Jewish blood

For us, one of the most compelling insights from the teachings of the Talmud is that this religious law was actually able to guarantee Judaism an astonishingly high degree of purity in its racial composition. Adolf Hitler says in *Mein Kampf*:

> Jewish religious doctrine is primarily a collection of instructions for maintaining the blood purity of Jewry, and for regulating intercourse between Jews, themselves, and

---

[16] For a concise, classic analysis of the Shulchan Aruch, and related Talumdic concepts, see E. Bischoff, *The Book of the Shulchan Aruch* (2023).

the rest of the world—which is to say, their relation with non-Jews.[17]

It must be recognized that no other European religion has, in its teachings, advocated for the question of keeping the blood pure in this form— nor could it do so, in this manner and structure.

---

[17] *Mein Kampf*, vol. 1, sec. 11.13, p. 308.

## — 3 —
# JUDAISM AMONG THE RACES

### 19. The first Jewish migrations

With the law of their God Yahweh in their hearts, the Jews were scattered among the peoples of the world in migrations lasting centuries, from time immemorial. Migrations in the Near East were followed by the invasion of Europe during the period of the Roman Empire. As early as the $2^{nd}$ century BC, Jews came to Crimea and the territory of the Khazars. It's not true, when the Jews claim that their great diaspora was ultimately caused by the destruction of the city of Jerusalem in the year 70. At that same time, the city of Alexandria was almost half-Jewish. Through it and other port cities, thousands of Jews spread to Greece, Italy, and the western Roman provinces.

According to Professor Seraphim, the root causes of Jewish migration, in addition to their expulsion from Palestine, were greatly influenced by the relocation of trade routes, by their own blood-based nomadic drive, and by their continued discernible foreignness to their environment. Or to put it another way: by their fundamental lack of inner ties to the spaces they inhabited.

### 20. The first appearance of Jews in Germany

At the beginning of our common era, the number of Jews still living in Palestine is estimated at 700,000, while the number living in the diaspora—that is, in the dispersion—were already estimated at 3.5 million. The expansion of the Roman Empire gave Jews an opportunity to reach "southern Spain, into Gaul on the Germanic frontier, even as far as the Lower Rhine and into Britain." They are documented in "Trier around 275; in Cologne there was a firmly organized Jewish community recorded in 321 and 331." Already in Sulla's time, it was said that it was hard to find a place that had welcomed this people in and then not been taken over by them. While 500 years before there were at most half a million Jews, by the time of the Caesars, the number had grown to five million, some seven percent of the total population. (For comparison: in Frankfurt am Main, Jews were 4.7% of the population in 1925.)[18]

## 21. The destruction of the Greco-Roman cultural world by the Jews

While the Jews had already penetrated the Greek cultural world, their intrusion into the Roman Empire was the most consequential development. Firmly established since the heyday of the Caesars, the Jews had an unbridled hatred of the Roman Empire, which was established according to healthy blood and racial views. We can already see from these examples from earlier times that everything good and noble has always had an instinctive opponent in the Jew. Even though he is a hideous mongrel, he seeks to preserve the existing substance of his blood with artificial laws. Perhaps the most profound realization is that the preservation of his present blood mixture only preserves the characteristic traits of his nature: hence the malefactor's will to self-assertion.

True to their nature, the Jews of Rome were able to assert themselves as market speculators or even as major bankers. A papyrus from the year 41 survives in which an Alexandrian merchant advises his indebted business friend: "Beware of the Jew." However, the Jews understood how to make themselves indispensable, so that they increasingly penetrated into the leading state positions of the Roman Empire and asserted their influence. Nero's wife, Poppaea Sabina, was a follower of Judaism. Under Trajan (98 to 112 AD), the complaint has been preserved: "It is painful to us that your Council of State is full of Jews!"

The edicts that were issued to the Jews by the late Roman emperors for their protection and privilege are largely still preserved. Under Emperor Caracalla (212), all Jews were granted Roman citizenship. An early Roman poet of the 1st century complained that the Rome of his day was not animated by its own citizens, but by "the yeast of the globe." Another says: "Being Roman means nothing anymore; only those who recently arrived in Rome on the Syrian ships lay on couches dressed in Tyrian robes."

Once in possession of influential positions, the Jews immediately used their newly-gained power to internally contaminate and disintegrate

---

[18] According to *Europe and the East*, published by Hans Hagemeyer and Dr. Georg Leibbrandt.

the idea of the Roman state with their Oriental notions. Absolutism, universalism, and Asiatic theocracy became the new models for the Roman Empire. Under this influence, a human slurry gradually emerged with an international cultural and religious establishment, which ultimately—with the exception of Judaism, which consciously stayed out of it—smothered every ethnic peculiarity and brought about the downfall of the Empire from within. No less than Theodor Mommsen calls the Jews in antiquity "an effective ferment of national decomposition."[19]

Their behavior was among the most striking in the former Roman province of Spain, which was conquered by Germanic tribes, mainly the Visigoths, in the 5th century. Sensing their advantage, namely good business, the Jews immediately sided with their new masters, only to betray them again later with an equal lack of compunction. As is well known, they provided every possible assistance to the Arabs from North Africa who were advancing across the Strait of Gibraltar against the Visigothic Kingdom.[20]

## 22. Privileges consolidated the position of the Jews in Germanic lands

Jews migrated to German territories primarily in the wake of the Roman Legions. Quite early on, Charlemagne [circa 800 AD] and his successors gave special privileges to the Jews. This was based not only on the moral and intellectual grounds of Christianity, which was expanding at that time, but also out of utilitarian considerations, which arose due to Jews' domination of the currency market under the German emperor. We see again and again the typical scenario of how the Jews, using every conceivable masquerade, suck up the wealth of the peoples: they endeavor to make themselves useful, they point out that they have connections everywhere, and then they put the wealth they have accumulated to work.

In the minds of the targeted peoples, these activities serve their own interests, but in reality, it is done only for the ruthless enrichment of the Jews on the wealth of their hosts until it is completely swallowed up.

---

[19] *The History of Rome* (1856/1871), p. 643.
[20] For details, see *Weltkampf* 1941, issue 1/2, p. 8.

## 23. New trade routes promote the further spread of Judaism

In time, Judaism spread in rapid succession to North Africa and Spain, Portugal, Holland, and finally to England and France; at the same time, it also penetrated into southeastern Europe.[21]

During the 12th to the 16th centuries, Judaism experienced a major shift from west to east caused by a wide variety of factors, such as renewed expulsions and rebellions by the aggrieved peoples. But particularly significant was the realization that the trade routes of southeastern Europe brought rich profits; and finally, that the nature of southeastern Europeans, especially the Slavic peoples, allowed Jews to live out their lives with less constraint than was possible in western and central Europe. Over time, eastern Jewry thus became the strongest group of world Jewry, able to repeatedly provide fresh blood to the Jewish world.

## 24. The expulsion of the Jews

We now arrive at the ample history of Jewish expulsions; we will refer to only a few of the basic facts. Among other things, Jews were purged in:

    855—from the Italian city-states
    1096—from Trier, Speyer, Mainz, and Cologne
    1181—from France
    1290—from England
    1306—again from France
    1492—from Spain.[22]

In the later Middle Ages, Jews were also often expelled from German lands. The lack of sufficient central authority left it to the cities and states to determine and carry out these necessary measures. Cologne commenced for this reason in 1424, Mainz and Strasbourg in 1438, Augsburg in 1430, Bavaria in 1450, Silesia in 1455, Erfurt in 1458, Tirol in 1499, and Regensburg in 1519. In addition to these principal expulsions, there

---

[21] See also Rosenberg, *The Track of the Jew Through the Ages.*
[22] According to Seraphim: *Migrations of the Jewish People.*

were many more that cannot be listed.[23] It is worth mentioning on this subject that the Church often played a leading or supporting role in the expulsion of the Jews. The prevailing view of the Church was that the Jews were guilty of the death of Christ, which gave the church a reason for its actions, but also the fact that it often made itself the spokesman for the general repudiation of the Jews, who were perceived as "different."

## 25. The Jew invades England

The renewed penetration of Judaism into England is particularly remarkable. The immigration of, firstly, individuals and then numerous Jews to England was deliberately carried out when the Spanish, Portuguese, and Dutch colonial powers were displaced by the English, and England began to build up its empire. The resistance of the English population was ignored by its government. And it was Oliver Cromwell, in particular, who, based on his Puritan views stemming from the Old Testament, believed that he had to allow the Jews back into England. Undoubtedly, Cromwell also though of putting the Jews' global trade relations in the service of English colonial power.

From that time onward, England, along with all of its colonies, was at the mercy of Judaism. For many years, England offered the parasitic character of the Jew the best breeding ground, based on the ideological attitude of its residents and the resulting conditions of its economy, its trade, and its idea of political rule.

## 26. Do the Jews have a home country?

Is there, one may ask, an actual native homeland for the Jews? The brief depiction of the Jewish diaspora presented here does not yet answer this crucial question. Ferdinand Fried, in his book *The Ascent of the Jews*, offers a response:

> They have no roots in any country, but they proliferate everywhere, and in this way they have a destructive effect on

---

[23] Refer to Siefert: *The Jew on the Eastern Border*. This book provides extraordinarily interesting insight into the nature of eastern Jewry.

every host nation like a parasitic bacteria. Yet this corrosive force only became decisively operative when the commercial system of usury was combined with a religion that was tailored to it. Regarded from this point of view, the nature of the Jewish faith resides in the fact that its followers do not need a homeland, but content themselves with the more theoretically understood 'Jerusalem' ('there looming in the light'). This conforms to their rootlessness.

Furthermore, their law, the Torah, provides the spiritual bond that connects together firmly all racial and religious kin, even if they are homeless and scattered all over the world. Ultimately, the power inherent in this expanding faith favored the racial kinsmen. With an implacable ruthlessness and passionate hatred of everything foreign (particularly their foreign host people, the goyim), Judaism promoted the dispersion of its followers all over the Earth, their continued cohesion and, above all, the ethical demand to subvert the loathsome outsider.

## 27. The Ghetto

With the declaration of fundamental human rights in the American House of Representatives and in the French National Assembly, the last barriers that stood in the way of equality for the Jews were removed. The French Revolution, which involved the peoples of the entire European continent, created the conditions for the complete emancipation of Europe's Jews in the course of the 19th century.

This emancipation was associated with the abolition of the ghettos everywhere. Originally, the ghettos were a self-imposed arrangement by Jewry in order to have a living area in which they could fully pursue their own customs. Over time, however, the ghettos increasingly became a rule of the host peoples. Thus they represented an instinct of defense by the host against Jewish attempts at assimilation. The abolition of the ghettos subsequently helped to obscure the distinctiveness of the Jews. In the end, only Eastern Europe had natural ghettos, just as the crime districts of the major cities all over the world can also be described as natural ghettos. We can certainly take the view that, even today around the world, Judaism is still recruited from the anti-social elements of all peoples.

How much the emancipation of the Jews corresponded to the short-sightedness of the host peoples, rather than to the wishes of the Jews, is described in a passage from the novel *Endymion*, written by the English Jew Benjamin Disraeli, the later Earl of Beaconsfield:

> No man will treat with indifference the principle of race. It is the key of history, and why history is often so confused is that it has been written by men who were ignorant of this principle and all the knowledge it involves. ... But the Semites now exercise a vast influence over affairs by their smallest though most peculiar family, the Jews. There is no race gifted with so much tenacity, and such skill in organisation. These qualities have given them an unprecedented hold over property and illimitable credit. ... But what do they mean by the Latin race? Language and religion do not make a race—there is only one thing which makes a race, and that is blood.[24]

Liberalism did not want to see any of this, and it was only the Führer who clearly pointed out, on the subject of Judaism among the people, that the Jew and the world-Bolshevism that they enabled, were utterly foreign contaminants.

## 28. The overseas emigration of the Jews

The discovery of America for their purposes by the Jews around 1830, and especially from 1870 onwards, initiated their overseas emigration.[25] Jews estimate that in the century between 1830 and 1930, 4.2 million of their number emigrated overseas, 2.9 million of them to the United States alone. It is striking that this figure includes 1.7 million Jews just from Russia. It is not difficult to see that these elements can easily bring into the American race not only a general disfigurement and racial degrada-

---

[24] Chapter 56.
[25] According to Seraphim, op. cit.

tion, but also the high degree of Jewish-Bolshevist character displayed by the present American leaders, to the applause of their followers.

The fact that 15 percent of the Jews living in Germany in 1933 were still foreign-born shows just how much Jewish migration is still going on today. The caution not to settle down too firmly and to retain mobility prompted 23 percent of all Jews living in Germany at that time to obtain or use a foreign citizenship, just to be on the safe side, in addition to their German citizenship.

## 29. Palestine as a Jewish state

Despite all these migrations, the shifting back and forth from occupation to occupation, some Jews still have not given up the idea of a Jewish homeland that can also be represented in physical territory. Chaim Weizmann, born in 1875, together with the Jew Nahum Sokolow, was the originator of the Balfour Declaration, according to which Palestine was proclaimed the Jewish national homeland. One should not be mistaken about the so-called Zionist movement. It is the leading trend among Jewry. And even if, according to previous experience, it is less likely that Palestine will represent a centrally-acting force for all of Judaism, than merely a pathetic self-satisfied thought-game, the Zionist Jews are nevertheless the tone-setters of world Jewry.[26]

## 30. The Soviet Jewish Republic of Birobidzhan

The inability of the Jews to create "homeland" in our sense also applies to the experiences that were made with the Jewish quasi-autonomous Soviet Republic of Birobidzhan. Allotted to the Jews as early as 1918, this region in the south of Siberia, which was predominantly covered by forest and incredibly rich in other natural resources, proved to be unviable, even though it was proclaimed a state within the USSR in 1934. Here the Jews could have demonstrated, in an area much more fertile

---

[26] Zionist goals were attained just a few years after this writing, as the UN endorsed the idea of a Jewish homeland in Palestine, and the subsequent creation of the state of Israel. Today, nearly all Jews worldwide are Zionists, in that they support the existence of the state of Israel—even if it demands the ethnic cleansing of indigenous Arabs.

than Palestine could ever be, that they were serious about creating a nation state. The Soviets had given the Jews of Birobidzhan all the rights that could only be granted in the USSR. And although major support measures were announced for Jews willing to migrate and settle, only a few tens of thousands moved to this country. Most of those Jews, who at first could hardly protect themselves from the desire to own land, soon left this country again. This correlates with the response of a Jew, who, when asked about the reasons for his departure from Birobidzhan, said: "Why should I live so hard in the countryside, when I can live so much easier in the city?"

Nevertheless, as already mentioned, the Zionist movement has one characteristic that should not be overlooked: Even if it was not able to convince all Jews of the need for their own state, it nevertheless became the recognized representative of world Jewry in the sense of creating a single intellectual home for the basis of Jewish orthodoxy. The Zionist movement feels itself to be the leader of the genuine heritage of the forefathers, and it is a fact that most of the leading Jews emerge from its ranks.

With these goals, it is also the real proxy of Jewish parasitism. There are probably only a few eligible heads of state in the world who have not yet been "honored" with a declaration of loyalty from the Zionist Jews, a vow that lasted only until the parasite took hold. But then the allegiance disappeared and gave way to a multitude of demands, among which the demand for 'equality' was, and is, only a poorly disguised claim to their desired autocracy.

# — 4 —
# THE JEWISH WORLD-PARASITE
# IN THE BLOODSTREAMS AND ORGANS
# OF THE NATIONS

## 31. The creeping poison

The brief review of Jewish migrations showed that over the centuries, but especially during the liberalist 19th century, Jews mixed with all the major peoples of the world. It is now necessary to pinpoint the manner in which Judaism has parasitically embedded itself into the bloodstreams and organs of the individual peoples. Outwardly, this seemed to happen more or less inconspicuously in most cases, due to the clever exploitation of circumstances. As Houston Stewart Chamberlain already remarked in his *Foundations of the 19th Century*:

> Determined by ideal motives, the Indo-European opened the gates in friendship: the Jew rushed in like an enemy, stormed all the positions and planted—I don't want to say in the rubble, but on the breaches of our genuine individuality—the flag of his being, which is eternally alien to us.[27]

In *Mein Kampf*, the Führer describes for us the manner in which the Jew crept into the bloodstream of the people and worked to gain power and sway.[28] In summary: First, the Jew comes as a trader, then he begins to work in the economy, not as a producer, but as an intermediate link, and he lends money at usurious interest rates. Then he settles down and sees trade and financial transactions as a privilege, which he expands into a monopoly. Wherever people have become acquainted with the parasitic nature of the Jew and begin to harass him, he ingratiates himself to those in government, and endeavors to have them grant him special privileges to exploit the people. He also leads the princes to their ruin, by undermin-

---

[27] *Foundations of the 19th Century*, (1899/1911), pp. 330-331.
[28] *Mein Kampf*, vol. 1, sec. 11.15 ("The Way of Jewry"), pp. 310-318.

ing their position in relation to their subjects. And now, the Jew sees that his time has come to no longer regard himself as a foreigner within the framework of his host people, but rather to assimilate and rise to dominance. He flatters the population with his new ideas and new worldviews, and through his own art of lying makes himself the spokesman for a new age.

We have already referred to previous expulsions of the Jews, and we know from the history of the German Middle Ages that the Hohenstaufen Frederick II excluded Jews from all public offices; he pointed out that we find Jews wherever one is permitted to use violence, and consequently the Jew abuses it.[29]

## 32. National economy—Battlefield and domain of the Jews

Jewish influence became particularly strong with the dawn of the socalled era of high capitalism. The technological expansion that was initiated by the invention of the steam engine was accompanied by a material development that, in itself, in its beginning and in its effects, need not have been in any way harmful to the German national soul or to the German people, if it had been captured and controlled by our own forces. But in just a few decades, the battlefield of the economy became the domain of Judaism. Here, for the first time, the Jew was able to apply his centuries-old practices of money management on a large scale, especially since the emerging liberalist view opened all doors and gateways for him.

## 33. The Jews gain equal rights

The French Revolution of 1789 and, before that, the Congress of the United States of America, proclaimed the equal rights of the Jews by including in their laws the principle of the equality of all races and peoples. In what was then Germany, the so-called emancipation movement came into currency at about the same time in both Prussia and Austria. In Berlin, it was Moses Mendelssohn (Ben Menachem Mendel) in particular, who was born in Dessau in 1729 and died in Berlin in 1786. He is rightly called the father of Jewish emancipation in Germany. The Jewish

---

[29] *Foundations*, p. 345.

Prof. Dr. Grätz described him as a man who, to a certain extent, represented the image of this tribe, and was crooked in shape, clumsy and unattractive in appearance.

But Mendelssohn was by no means intellectually graceless; rather, he sought to gain a foothold in Berlin's leading society and succeeded in doing so to an astonishing degree. His goal was to pave the way for fellow members of his race to achieve personal freedom within their host nation. At his instigation, the war councilor Christian Dohm (1751-1820) wrote the memorandum "On the Civil Improvement of the Jews" in 1781. While Dohm's presence in Alsace and his own pro-Jewish attitude had already led him to advocate for the improvement of the situation of Alsatian Jews, this treatise became a matter of concern for Jews throughout Europe. Prince Carl August von Hardenberg (1750-1822), minister of the Prussian state in his early years, was greatly influenced by Mendelssohn's ideas and also by Dohm's writings in a pro-Jewish manner. He was also certainly forced to adopt this attitude by the fact that Samson and Israel Jacobson, the Braunschweig court Jews, were the main financial donors for the minister, who was almost constantly in financial difficulties. He repaid this courtesy with political favors.

Against the resistance of many clear-thinking people in the Prussian state at the time, Hardenberg pushed through the famous Jewish Edict of 11 March 1812, according to which Jews were now equal to Prussian citizens in their rights and duties. Even though this proclamation on the civil circumstances of Jews was a good precursor, and even though the Enlightenment and Liberalism helped clear the way, many misgivings remained in Prussia about the declaration of equal rights for Jews. After all, Jews still had no opportunity to enter the civil service after this edict, and they also remained excluded from many other public offices. The last barriers in this regard fell on 3 July 1869, when complete equality for Jews in these matters was enshrined in Prussian state law. The only profession to which Jews were not admitted was that of officer. This exception was strictly observed in all northern German states, and even in the southern German states, it was only possible for one or two Jews to become professional officers.

What good was it, that many great Germans in their time had spoken out against the Jews? When Luther in his *Table Talk* said: "Therefore, know thou, dear Christian, and do not doubt that next to the devil you will not find a more bitter, more poisonous, more savage enemy than the Jew who seriously wants to be a Jew…" and further gave the German people advice on how to defend themselves against the Jews—advice that leaves nothing to be desired in terms of clarity. When Frederick the Great and Goethe turned against the Jews, or when Fichte says:

> Through almost all the countries of Europe a powerful hostile state is spreading, which is constantly at war with all the others, and which in some ways puts a terrible heavy pressure on its citizens: it is Judaism.[30]

All these voices had to fade away now, that the state had granted the Jews equal rights.

The same development took place in the Austrian monarchy, the other major representative of the German race at that time, in the face of sometimes quite serious resistance by the German population.

## 34. The Jew with equal rights as the destroyer of the people's natural order of life

As mentioned above in the Führer's description of the way Jews insinuated themselves into the bloodstream of the people, after capturing the governments, the Jews now wanted to conquer the very soul of the people. It is no wonder then that the numerical increase in the working class, which went hand in hand with industrialization, effectively invited the Jew to secure the dominant influence on the workers' movement. Short-sightedly, the government and the bourgeoisie were unable to do anything with the new social class of factory workers at the time. They were alien to this modern mass movement, incapable of making the organically-correct decisions that were necessary according to the laws of blood.

While the Prussian workers' movement was still initially an attempt to bring the emerging mass of workers into "harmony" with the people as a whole, Judaism did everything in its power to oust from their posts as quickly as possible the first leaders of the German workers' movement who represented such ideas, and to make it impossible for the workers to

---

[30] 1793; reproduced in T. Dalton, *Eternal Strangers* (p. 78).

follow them. In the decisive years surrounding the 1848 Revolution, we see that Jewish influence on the leadership of the labor movement became established in the strongest possible way.

### 35. Judaism installs itself at the top of the labor movement

We now encounter the names of Moses Hess of the *Rheinischen Zeitung* in Cologne; Karl Marx, editor-in-chief of this newspaper; Karl Isidor Beck, the so-called "poet of the poor"; and the Jews Karl Grün, Dr. Johann Jacoby, Karl Ludwig Bernays, Heinrich Heine, and German Mäurer. In Berlin, the labor movement was led by Stephan Born (Simon Buttermilch), originally an artisan in Berlin; he subsequently became a professor at the University of Basel and editor of the *Baseler Nachrichten*. Finally, we should not forget Ferdinand Lassalle (Loslauer, Lasel, Lasal), who later was killed in a duel.

Bernays and Heine, together with Marx and Hess, published the *German Yearbooks* in the 1840s. When these were no longer allowed to be published, Hess, Marx, Heine, and Mäurer were involved in the founding of *Vorwärts* ("Forward!") in Paris in 1844—a founding that would not last a year. Nevertheless, it is not without a certain pungency that Giacomo Meyerbeer (Jacob Liebmann Meyer Beer), who was the Prussian Director of Music at the time, contributed 3,000 francs to the founding funds. How much effort must it have cost Meyerbeer to finally become Royal Prussian General Director of Music? He thought it proper though, once he held that position, to provide funds to establish a German newspaper abroad that was agitating against his own government.

### 36. *The Communist Manifesto*—Judaism declares war on the world

Marx played the largest part in creating a programmatic statement about the inner nature of the labor movement. It is principally to him, a son of the Mordecai family of rabbis in Trier, that we owe the *Communist Manifesto*, this declaration of war against the whole world. Marx's hatred of his own country of birth was so great that he quite openly stated in his manifesto that Germany would be one of the first countries in which communism would flourish.

The Jews succeeded in uniting the Labor movement of the time under the banner of communism, in disrupting the healthy nationalistic attitudes of the people, and inspiring in them a hatred for all existing order. Through their attitudes, the apolitical bourgeoisie of the period always gave the communists the best opportunities to rebel against the prevailing conditions. A lack of sophistication, a deficient basic ideological attitude, and a political obtuseness made the position of the bourgeoisie increasingly weak, and at the same time strengthened the position of the communists.

If the worker was aroused by communism to have material hopes that could never be fulfilled, the Jewish world-parasite recognized in this another useful tool for making himself master of the world. The Jew, whose cosmopolitan thinking gave rise to the idea of world supremacy, aspired to take possession of all the world's wealth and labor power. He sought to achieve this goal by causing disruption of the economy, through fragmentation of the individual sectors and through the incitement of particular sectors of the population against each other. National economies should disappear; and the first outlines of world plutocracy under Jewish leadership began to emerge.

These deeply Jewish plans of subversion were carried out using every possible means with the greatest ruthlessness. The individual races were led from revolution to revolution, subjected to one political or economic convulsion after another. The fact that this intentionally planned disorganization of the national structures of power did not succeed even faster than anticipated, is due to the yet-enduring power of the people.

### 37. "Everything German works on me like an emetic"

It is necessary, in this brief review of the evolution of the German labor movement, to emphasize once again the genuine mindset of Judaism towards the national interests of its host peoples on the basis of individual Jewish testimonies. Heinrich Heine once said: "Everything German works on me like an emetic." In our time, Bernard Baruch, an advisor to Franklin Roosevelt, said: "I think national pride is a bunch of nonsense" (according to Leers).

The more Judaism had its sway within the labor movement and the more Jews became its leaders over the decades, the more apparent this attitude became. For example, at the Essen party conference of 1907,

Karl Liebknecht, who was Jewish, expanded on the above-mentioned statements and added: "We want the proletariat repulsed by military drills; we are happy if discipline in the army is not as good as within the Social Democratic Party." The Jew Ernst Heilmann told the magazine *Das Frei Wort* (according to Leers): "Away with the songs that glorify the national community and the nation state, away with the *Deutschland-lied* (the German National Anthem)." And lastly, as early as 1903, the Jew Eckstein said: "Behind the general conflict must be the will for a decisive battle."

So even back then, it was possible to dare to speak publicly of an imminent decisive battle. And what should this decisive battle be about? The misguided German worker believed that he would receive an improvement in his wages, and particularly, an improvement in his social standing—at least, that is how the Jew presented it to him. For him as a Jew, however, these are trivialities. For him, it's a matter of having the masses of workers who would fight for his goals: namely the destruction of every economy and general violence in order to establish Jewish world domination.

## 38. The bourgeoisie fails

As mentioned already, there is no longer any doubt that the attitude of the bourgeoisie and the leading classes only supported this double game played by the Jew and his workers. Houston Chamberlain refers to the accomplices of the Jews from the ranks of the princes and the nobility, "who have always, for the most despicable reasons, encouraged, protected, and promoted the destructive activities of the Jews." The Führer and Alfred Rosenberg tell us something similar. The bourgeoisie, nourished by the views of the Christian denominations, has not, to this day, allowed itself to see Judaism as a racial enemy, but only as a special type of religious community.

## 39. Jewish blood seeps into German families

Liberal ideas, combined with the emancipation laws, made it possible for Judaism to penetrate the bourgeois world in blood. When equal rights for the Jews were declared, Jews began to marry into German families. And we know today to what extent Jews prevailed, not only in penetrating into the oldest aristocratic families in Germany, but also into the nobility in general and the leading spiritual, economic, and administrative families in Germany. In doing so, the Jew consolidated his power in a wide variety of areas, and the blood of many German families was contaminated for all time.

The National Socialist German people have inherited a bitter legacy from their fathers in this area. For it will take many decades until the consequences of this Russian invasion of the Jews in our blood can be overcome. Today, not a few German citizens remember with secret pride that some "famous" Jew once frequented their parents' home; and even if others believe they have to stand up for the Jews—because they aren't, or at least haven't been, "so bad"—this proves only too well how the liberal bourgeoisie of a racially-unenlightened period were exploited and seduced by the Jews, who were very conscious of their race.

### 40. Freemasonry as an organ of Judaism

Where the Jew was unable to penetrate an individual German family directly, he succeeded by use of the social clubs and through Freemasonry in particular. This institution, in the course of its history, has proven to be the best breeding ground for Jewish influence to flourish and mature to the highest levels of success. How flattered the individual German citizen felt when he was asked to take part in the meetings of the lodges, and when he felt that they intended to accept him. How much worry, how much disappointment and bitterness, entered the hearts of many German men when they later discovered, as lodge members, the shackles with which they were now bound to this Jewish Freemasonry.

How much stupid pride and how much arrogance, on the other hand, were also developed by German men who, as willing lodge brothers, quashed the voice of their blood and their souls, and completely succumbed to the whispers of Jewish-Masonic leadership.

### 41. Jewish dictatorship of the press

The press was a particular area of influence for the Jews. It too was skillfully used to influence the public opinion of the host nations in the service of Jewish interests. It would be foolish to assume that the Jew only had his say in the so-called inflammatory press. But he was just as interested and invested in the bourgeois national newspapers. Like fire and water, a paper might ostensibly give the impression of a certain orientation, but in the background, there were still Jewish advisors, publishing directors, or financiers, who, contrary all the solemn struggle on display, ensured that the interests of Judaism were taken into account on all points.

With the help of the dictatorship of the press, Judaism was able to bludgeon everything spiritually, and saw the most respectable Germans, inspired by the purest will, defamed in the press like they were the worst criminals of the century. To suddenly fall prey to public contempt or to encounter public distrust, even if it was just caused by an inconspicuous notice in the Jewish press, meant your life was made impossible; you were "canceled".[31] As long as no newspaper thought of printing an apology, quite apart from the fact that harm had already occurred, the consequences of the slander were by no means eliminated.

Through the press, Judaism also had the power to shape the individual German's ideal image of life. Spiritual disintegration through editorials and other contributions was followed by material disintegration. Articles or advertisements were used, as the Jew said, to keep the economy going—that is, to promote spending or the desire to buy very specific items. In reality, however, the desire to buy was directed by the cleverly managed advertising not only to really necessary things, but also to all sorts of things that no average German household needed.

## 42. Judaism and the Parties

The political parties were another means by which world Jewry enforced its political will. If Imperial Germany already had a number of parties and, in the period of decline, there were many more, sometimes over 30, then this was rarely necessary. Instead, this was the natural consequence of Jewish destruction, Jewish deception, and Jewish lies. What could be more pleasing to the Jew, than a German nation divided into many parties. Here, too, the Jew did not mind seeing himself represented in *all* the

---

[31] A remarkable anticipation of today's "cancel culture."

parties, as much as possible. This prevailed from the Social Democratic Party to the Conservative Party.

And if the lone German believed that the Jew in his party had made it his mission to pursue the stated goals of that very party, then he was hugely mistaken. Because here too, Jews' commitment to their own community, to their feeling of belonging together, was stronger than their commitment to established party programs. As a Jew, he had only one interest: to ensure that Jewish plans did not somehow come up short.

### 43. The entrance of the Jews into culture

How Judaism nested itself into all areas of culture! Theater, cinema, even all branches of music and the performing arts were appropriated by them as well. His nimble intellect, which was only capable of imitation, enabled him to shine in all areas. However, the Jew was unable to create anything truly new. The propaganda that he put up as a substitute for Jewish art concealed this deficiency. And using all the possibilities of politics, the press, and finance, the Jew touted Jewish artists to the German people as the only true ones, as the real role models to which no other mortal in this world could aspire.

### 44. The "heyday" of Judaism during the period of German decline

The heyday of the Jews seemed to begin when they succeeded in coming to power via the German Social Democrats in 1918. As early as 1911, Karl Liebknecht, a communist related to Judaism by marriage, said: "In the event of war, we will use all means of force at our disposal to seize the government of the Empire." And it's not surprising that in March 1915, Jewish members of the then-Social Democratic faction voted against the approval of further war loans: Bernstein, Davidson, Fuchs, Geyer, Haase, Herzfeld, Hoch, Stadthagen, Cohn, and the Jew-connected Liebknecht. During the war, the Jew Walter Rathenau organized the so-called War Raw Materials Department, which soon achieved the absolute disorganization of economic life. Together with the arms and ammunition procurement offices, an ample number of lucrative positions were provided for Jews behind the front lines.

When the Imperial German government was supported, as 25 November 1918, the German federal states were represented in the Berlin government by the following Jews: Adler, Bernstein, Cohn, Eisner, Flieder, Gradnauer, Haase, Haas, Hirsch, Heymann, Herzfeld, Löwengart, Oberländer, Preuß, Rosenfeld, and Wurm. With them came all the Jewish fraudsters, some of whom the German people had gotten to know from the great racketeering and usury trials of the 1920s: Sklarek, Sklarz, Holzmann, Kutisker, Barmat, and comrades.

One of the most influential Jews in the field of economic policy was Jacob Goldschmidt. After becoming the managing director of the Darmstadt and National Bank, he was able to unify control of 104 supervisory board positions as well as his own bank management duties. In 1927, "On account of his tangible services to Reconstruction," he was made an honorary Doctor of Political Science. How great his contributions to the reconstruction really were could be gauged in 1931 when the bank he headed was so wrecked by mismanagement that the German Reich was forced to guarantee it through a special emergency decree on 13 July 1931. Because of this, few people in Germany fell into economic ruin, while only eight years previously, the entire German people had been reduced to begging by the inflation caused and exploited by Judaism.

We are all still familiar with how much Judaism at this time overturned the fields of art and culture. We need only remember the Rotter Brothers stage in Berlin, the revues of James Klein, composers like Korngold and Schreier, the violinist Fritz Kreisle, the writers Lion Feuchtwanger, Egon Erwin Kisch, Ernst Toller, and others.

Another particularly effective resource for Jews, that of medicine, must be mentioned in this context. Of the approximately 50,000 licensed doctors in Germany, 6,488 were Jews: some 13 percent. The Jewish doctors made themselves the spokesmen for free love and all manner of sexual aberrations. Thusly, they had secured an acutely potent position for their parasitic activities, and admittedly they achieved a great deal.

At this time, however, when Judaism felt it held sway in politics, economics, and the arts, and was firmly convinced that it had already made great progress towards the domination of the German people—as Jews were police chiefs or assistant chiefs, ministers, and anything was possible—that the German people, under the decisive sole leadership of Adolf Hitler's National Socialist German Workers' Party, rose up against

Judaism. They did so to such an extent that, in the midst of this feeling of victory, the Jews completely dropped their mask in defense of the position they had achieved. Until then, Jews had repeatedly persuaded the German people that they only wanted what was best for them. Now their abysmal hatred for a people that had still not submitted was revealed; the desire for the absolute destruction of the German essence. The world of the ideas of Bolshevism, which arose from Marxist-Communist doctrine, was systematically transferred to Germany by the Jews, and a path was cleared for it to be effective, in order for it to be an auxiliary force with which one could win in Germany.

Furthermore, every means was used to turn the world against Germany. And while the newly emerging young nation had the best will to live in harmony with all peoples of the world, the Jewish press before and after 1933 unanimously portrayed it as the eternal troublemaker, one whose Teutonic belligerence could never be escaped. The more the Jews realized that their strong position in Germany was wavering, the more they sowed hatred against Germany and tried to promote the work of extermination.

The Führer repeatedly pointed out this Jewish incitement in speech and writing, and wrote the following sentences in *Mein Kampf*:

> Hence it is that the Jew today is the great agitator for the complete destruction of Germany. Whenever in the world we read of attacks against Germany, Jews are their fabricators. In peacetime and during the War, Jewish stock-exchange and Marxist press systematically stirred up hatred against Germany, until one state after another abandoned its neutrality and placed itself at the service of the world war coalition, renouncing the real interests of people.
>
> The Jewish way of reasoning thus becomes clear. The Bolshevization of Germany—that is, the rooting out of national folkish German intellectuals to make it possible for the German labor force to bear the yoke of Jewish world finance —is only a prelude to an extension of the Jewish tendency for world conquest. As so often in history, Germany is the great pivot in this mighty struggle. If our people and our State should become victims of these bloodthirsty and ava-

ricious Jewish tyrants of nations, the whole Earth would fall prey to this polyp; and if Germany were to be freed from its grip, this greatest of dangers to nations would be broken for the whole world.[32]

## 45. The role of Judaism in other races

Just as with the German people, the Jew has established himself as a parasite in others races as well—to drain their national strength or to use it to serve his own purposes. Helmuth von Moltke already said in his description of the internal conditions in Poland:

> At all times, the Jews did not consider an oath in relation to a Christian to be binding… Even now, every city has its own judge, every province has its own rabbi, and all stand under an unknown head… All means are the same, as soon as what matters is earning money. In the campaign of 1812, the Jews were the spies, paid by both parties and expelled by both parties… It is strange that the police should cover up a theft in which no Jew was involved as an accomplice or as a fence.

As early as 1618, we know of a pamphlet from Krakow that complained about the decline of the city due to Jewish domination. What is interesting for us Germans is that the Polish author of this work still vividly remembers Krakow's German past and Krakow's lively cultural and economic connections to the German Empire. The same author also eloquently describes the methods by which the Jew conducts his business.

Over the centuries, the Jew has become more and more entrenched in the Polish national body. He dominated trade to the widest extent; they were to be found in all branches of the economy, from the simplest to the leading activities; they were as much members of the proletariat in Poland as members of society. Instead of making use of the opportunities given to them for positive achievement, they were obedient tools in the

---

[32] *Mein Kampf*, vol. 2, sec. 13.10 (pp. 253-254).

hands of world Jewry. Thus it was the Jews who led the Polish state into the abyss of state destruction.

In France, the following picture emerged: The prospect of active civil rights for the Jews was the work of Berr Isaac Berr from Nancy, who led a delegation to the French government and remained there with it until 14 October 1789, when the desired resolution by the National Assembly on equal rights was achieved. What did it matter to the Jews that one of the conditions imposed on them for this granting of civil rights was the reduction of the Alsatian population's debt to the Jews by two-thirds? The Jews had experienced such a reduction in guilt too often not to know that the new rights they had acquired would make them much richer than they could have been if they had remained second-class citizens.

A few decades later, Napoleon commented on his experience with the Jews as follows:

- "Since the time of Moses, the Jewish nation has been based on usury and extortion."
- "The Jews are not in the same position as the Protestants and the Catholics. They must be judged according to constitutional law, not civil law, since they are not citizens."
- "The Jews have supplied provisions for my armies in Poland; I want to give them a political existence in return, I want to make them into a nation and citizens; but they are good for nothing but haggling over old clothes. I was forced to pass laws against their usury, and the peasants in Alsace thanked me for it."

Another Frenchman, Henri de Rochefort (1830-1913), said:

The Jews are to blame for all the great catastrophes of my people. And that has always been the case in all countries and peoples that were forced to defend and protect themselves from the Jews. Within the liberal worldview, France became, from the middle of the last century, one of the main places of activity for the Jews. The uprisings of the Paris Commune of 1871, the various coup attempts, and the so-called image of public life were shaped, initiated, or largely influenced by them. The insignificance of the public resistance, and even the sympathy and support for the Jews by the bourgeoisie, which resulted from a complete misunderstanding of things, suited the intentions of Judaism. It quickly established itself in trade and the economy, and from then on corrupted the state until it either capitulated to the demands of the Jews or at least tried to save time and external reputation by changing ministers.[33]

If Poland, for world Jewry, was the point of departure for more economic, commercial, or pan-Slavic tendencies, the Jews of France tried for a long time, from Paris, to take advantage of liberalism, and to prepare for the fulfillment of world domination.

In 1923, the Führer said:

As Berlin agitated against Russia, so Paris agitated against Berlin. German miners rushed across the border to bring help to their French colleagues in a terrible disaster. Who crows the most hateful slander, who denigrates even this act, which springs from genuine German chivalry—*Matin*, *Journal*, and so on—but the entire Jewish press of France.

Once again, the clear visible ambition of world Jewry is to seek out and exploit conflicts.

We have also seen France almost fall to complete destruction at the hands of its Jewish and Masonic leaders in recent years. We need only think of the names Georges Mandel and Léon Blum. But now that France has fallen into misfortune, the Jews responsible have left their French "homeland" as far as this was still possible for them. They then tried to continue their old game, together with traitorous French generals—but not for the sake of the French nation, instead with France in the service of world Jewry.

We have already outlined the historical influence of Judaism in England. The fluctuating history of Jewish influence in England was followed by a

---

[33] According to Gregor Schwartz-Bostunitsch: *Jewish Imperialism*.

period from the 19<sup>th</sup> century onwards when Jewish influence became more and more prominent.

The social distress in the mother country of the British Empire, which was largely caused by the Jews—one thinks of the impoverishment of the English rural population, the labor conditions in mining and industry, but especially in the banking sector and the stock market—was something that was systematically manipulated to bring the English people under their rule. Agricultural work became unprofitable, and the rural population were advised to find work elsewhere in the economy. Workers were advised to work more, if they couldn't get by on their wages. Property owners were deprived of their money through bank and stock market manipulations or they were made dependent. In England, the doctrine of "free economy" developed, which became so free that it was impossible to see who was really leading the way to this freedom.

Thus, in the course of a few generations, in strict compliance with a law offered to the Jews by Englishmen with a Puritan-inspired mentality, and taking ruthless advantage of every possibility, all the characteristic features of Jewish foreign infiltration took place: action against state authority; substantial plundering of the host people through the destruction of the rural population; decomposition of racial consciousness; domination of the working population through indirect means; permanent interference in the governance of the state via the accumulated capital power. As a result, the focal point of Jewish power formation shifted from France to England. The keystone was the purification of the host people for Jewish world domination, and we will see in America, how far the individual plans have already progressed on the backs of the people.

It should be added here that it would be an aberration for the Jew to feel pity for the European peoples that he rules. Anyone who places himself in the hands of the Jews must know what danger this entails. For those who don't know this or don't want to know this, the words of the Jew Karl Emil Franzos apply: "Every people has the Jews it deserves."

Of the leading Jewish plutocratic houses in England, one is of particular interest: the House of Rothschild. From Germany, its path led simultaneously to Austria, France, and England. In a very short period of time, it established a predominant position of power in Europe, which was maintained until the 1940s essentially through a clever combination of matrimonial politics and the art of high finance. The path of the English Rothschilds is typical of the path of the Empire: their ancestor made money from Napoleon's defeat at Waterloo, the grandchildren made money from the English royal family, and the great grandchildren were prominently represented in the powerful Jewish class that surrounded Edward VII, who supported a policy of encirclement. Today's Rothschilds work to shift the center of Jewish power from England to America.

After all, it is no accident that it is the Jew who again today has led this English people to war against us. The Führer says:

> Back then, England was already our enemy. When I say 'England,' I know full well that the people and the leadership there are not one and the same. A small cabal of international democrats, Jews and plutocrats, dominates this country, and this clique was already inciting and agitating for war back then.

> Of course we now had to experience the same thing that we saw before the World War! As Germany rose, the envy of the same men who had already invaded Germany with war grew again. Mr. Churchill and his consortium immediately began to agitate again, which Mr. Eden and then of course the Jews, led by [Leslie] Hore-Belisha and others, began their agitation; and they increased it, year after year.

The United States of America and Russia are the two major landmasses in the world that have been most subject to the influences of Judaism so far. In both cases, the Jew was able to completely frustrate and disfigure the natural development of these peoples: the predominantly Germanic immigrant class in North America as well as the peoples of Russia. Here we are given clear examples of where people can end up if they do not find the strength to put a stop to the influence of Judaism in their ranks, before it is too late.

North America, the "Golden Land of Freedom"—or as it likes to call itself, "God's Own Country"—can claim the sad glory that American theater, American art, American culture, and American essence and existence in general, and in practice, have become far too closely interlaced with notions associated with the essence of Judaism. The guidebook *Europe and America* cites Henry Luce's statement that there is already enormous American internationalism today. American jazz, American films, American expressions, American machines and standard products are actually the only things that the entire world, from Zanzibar to Hamburg, recognizes in common. In such perceptions, which are widespread among the American population, the American desire for world domination is expressed. This desire is cleverly nurtured by the Jews, and is seen by them as one of the best launching pads for their own goals of world supremacy.

If, in the course of this war, we could hear Roosevelt's plans, which would be about controlled finance with a world currency—tied to the gold hoarded in America—and about a world bank organization that was supposed to be the intermediary for these financial plans (who wouldn't think of the notorious New York banking firm, Kuhn, Loeb & Co.), and spoke about an international food bank (the old Jewish plan of a centrally-controlled world food supply) and other world centers, then such plans only reveal, in a hidden way, genuinely Jewish plans and goals. With such intentions, the Jew can not only satisfy his addiction to expansion, his penchant for the collective, but at the same time rise to the highest possibility of human power: *world dictator*. Then he can rule and command, can take away the work, money, and even the food from those who are not completely devoted to him, then he can bring the whole of humanity into his sole dependence. Then, above all, Judaism can give free rein to its feelings of revenge against everything non-Jewish in this world; the great day that Yahweh had promised to his Jewish tribes would then come.[34]

By now, the Jew knows that an American century is not his own ultimate goal. But he will parasitically eat more and more into America, he will increasingly infiltrate and contaminate the entire American world, from the slums to the highest leadership, in order to use them to achieve his goals. He will tenaciously continue what he has been doing in America for decades. Already during the [First] World War (1914-1918), he seemed close to achieving his aims. The Führer said in 1923:

---

[34] As spoken by Malaysian prime minister Mahathir Mohamad in 2003: "Today the Jews rule the world by proxy [via America]. They get others to fight and die for them."

> After all, what reason did America have to go to war against Germany? Well, with the outbreak of the long-awaited world war, all major Jewish companies in the United States became war suppliers. They supplied the European war market to a degree that perhaps they had not even aspired to, and reaped a huge harvest! But that wasn't enough for the insatiable greed of the Jew. So the press, dependent on the stock market kings, began an unparalleled propaganda campaign. A gigantic organization of press lies was built.

The Jews had high hopes for Woodrow Wilson's plans; they also sent a whole series of representatives and advisors to the Wilson Peace Commission. When it did not come to fruition, American Jewry retreated to purely American concerns. The revival of interstate trade relations offered not only a lucrative, but also a well-camouflaged field of activity. Behind the scenes, however, the Jews Kahn, Warburg, the Schiff brothers, Guggenheim, Hanauer, and Breitung financed the Soviet revolution in Russia. This lucidly illustrates the age-old question of what the Jews do with the money they earn from their host peoples: they stir up the possibilities for world revolution.

Behind the Jewish bankers stands the Congress of American Jews, whose preliminary conference took place in Philadelphia on March 26 and 27, 1916. Some 367 delegates represented 4,381 associations. It was said then that this Congress "will make history not only for the Jewish people living in America, but throughout the entire world." This Congress counted among its founders Felix Frankfurter, who today is one of Roosevelt's most trusted collaborators, and who, through his clever personnel policy, brought numerous Jews into the top judicial positions in America and into Roosevelt's brain trust.

Jews also had an interest in replacing traditional agriculture in America with a new farming system. They financed farmers in order to unscrupulously expose smaller farms in favor of the larger ones, which in turn were exposed in favor of the giant farms. Mass production, money rush—these are things that can be recorded on the stock exchange, these are also the feelings of domination in the Jewish mind. The individual American's delight in technology was exploited and led to a kind of gigantomania, to the creation of giant corporations, all things, which apparently emphasize personality (think here of the "captains of industry"); but in reality, the personality of hundreds of thousands of others are reduced to insignificance, to the point of being a faceless mass of slaves. The glorification of the lives and successes of the few who reached the top was instrumentalized to drown out the countless forgotten disappointments of rest, to distract them and fill them with false hope.

From this constant harassment by the press, radio, industry, and the political parties, a way of life has arisen for the masses of Americans, who have become like sheep—a lifestyle for which we have coined the collective term 'gangsterism.' Gangsters, parasitical people living utterly destructively everywhere, building nothing, relying on robbery, theft, murder, and lies, despising all laws, without the dignity of someone enmeshed in the healthy inheritance of their race, but instead armed with all the impertinence of an atomized, spiritually-inert wretch. It causes us Europeans more than sadness when we see these descendants of our own ancestors at this low level of human life.[35] Yet this is not even the lowest level to which Jewish world domination would repress people. Russia offers an example of the worst possible outcome.

Russia in the hands of the Soviets is another prototype of the world state imagined by Jews. The methods by which they asserted themselves in Russia were, at the same time, a tremendous warning to many people worldwide. We can discern from what transpired there, the fate of complete debasement and destruction that threatens one's own people. In his work *Pestilence in Russia*, concerning Jewish leadership of the so-called Bolshevik revolution and the resulting Bolshevik state, Alfred Rosenberg communicates the following picture:

> It sounds implausible to world-weary Europeans, that this campaign against the intelligentsia of the people was carried out intentionally. By the beginning of 1922, 28 bishops, 1,215 clerics, over 6000 professors and teachers, almost 9000 doctors, 54,000 officers, 260,000 soldiers, al-

---

[35] A sad state of affairs, as acknowledged already in 1943; one can only imagine the further degree of American decay in the 80 years since then.

most 11,000 police officers, 58,500 constables, 12,950
landowners, 355,250 members of the intelligentsia,
193,350 workers, and 815,100 farmers fell victim to Soviet
"jurisdiction." Admittedly, a blind rage of destruction had
initially come over the Russian masses, still they were systematically incited to deprive themselves of the natural
leaders of their race. 'Divide and conquer' has always been
a military and political strategy; no one has pursued this
more consciously and dishonorably than the leaders of Bolshevism. If you deprive a race of the flowering of their spirit and intellect, they no longer exist as a people. All that
remains are the masses, which, if you understand its nature,
can be used for anything, at least temporarily.

And here we must touch on a point without which it is
completely impossible to understand Bolshevism: *Judaism.*
Such a systematic extermination of the national leadership
of Russia would never have occurred if Russians had been
at the forefront of this revolution. As it was, however, all
the anti-Russian groups and races treated this system of extermination that was established as a springboard to power,
and exploited it ruthlessly.

One need only mention that among the 550 Commissars
identified in 1921, there were 30 Russians, 34 Latvians, a
few Hungarians and Poles, and 447 Jews![36] This entire
swarm of Jewish criminals was welded together by instinct
and plan. By instinct, Jews recognized in Russia and in the
Russian people a principle at work that was antithetical to
their nature. Russians had still largely resisted attempts at
stock market exploitation that had achieved such brilliant
results in the West. This instinct, however, has long since
concentrated into a plan. I need not even refer to the hostile
"Protocols of the Elders of Zion".[37]

---

[36] For further details see, Rudolf Kommoss: *Juden hinter Stalin* (1942), and G.
von Poehl and M. Agthe: *Das Judentum, das wahre Gesicht der Sowjets*
(1942).
[37] See *Protocols of the Elders of Zion* (2023; Clemens & Blair).

After the death of international plutocrat Jacob Schiff himself, the Jews proudly shouted that he was the one who financed Japan's war against Russia, provided the prisoners of war with revolutionary propaganda, and that he was also behind the Russian Revolution of 1917. These things are so clear to everyone today that they do not require any further illustration. It should be noted that there were Bolshevik schools in all parts of Europe, for example in Zürich and on Capri. The Jews Rappoport, Mandelstamm, and Trotsky were famous teachers already long before the war.

These criminals had quite rightly said to themselves that any hope of success of leading the people and violating them can only happen if they are deprived of their leaders. For this reason and only for this reason, the worn-out, irritated, already half-crazy Russian was repeatedly whipped up into rage against his own blood through a series of ever-new propaganda measures. And in place of the expelled or murdered leadership stepped the Jewish conspirators. The art of seduction, cultivated over the centuries in Talmudic dialectics, is the essence of the Bolshevik method, and it is no coincidence that out of 51 press directors in Soviet Russia, 40 are Jews....

Of course, Jewish leadership in the capitals systematically ensured that Soviet representation abroad, that is, Jewish-Bolshevik foreign policy tools, were almost entirely in the hands of racial comrades.

The occupancy of the posts changes from time to time, with one agent giving up his position in Berlin to work for a while in Prague, Paris, or Warsaw, while the Bolsheviks there honored Germany in turn.

There can no longer be any doubt today about the planned implementation of a Jewish program by the presumptively non-racial Soviet government.

If we add to this the experiences made in Estonia, Latvia, and Lithuania after the Soviet occupation in 1940, which again consisted of the slaughter of tens of thousands of people in these countries with the best racial characteristics, then we see with full clarity the Jewish hatred of everything in this world exhibiting racial strength and health. It is an essential trait of Jewish Bolshevism that, in a kind of satanic calculation, it had many of its state-run capitalistic measures carried out by people it wanted to physically destroy with this work: the construction of the White Sea Canal, the Moscow Inland Sea, and the large armaments plants in Siberia are examples of this.

In the annihilation of all these peoples and ways of life, the Jew rises naked and exposed as ruler. He created state capitalism and thereby elevated the Soviet state to super-plutocrat status. He created the giant trusts and mega-projects, whose naming with popular names does not hide that fact that these are modern slavery operations. The person who works here is surrounded by all the external appearances of a free lifestyle, but he is only allowed to express himself collectively. Every opportunity to form a personality is blocked and every attempt to do so is punished. In doing so, the Jew created the mental bondage that manifests itself in the fundamental distrust inherent in every Soviet citizen. He may earn a living, he may be able to live in the cities partly in the European style, he may have state medals and awards—but mistrust remains his companion. He doesn't know what tomorrow will bring. He is at the mercy of a power that surrounds him, menacing and invisible, and which he feels sucking him dry until he either gives in or falls victim to extermination by a shot in the neck or deportation to a labor camp.

This completes the picture of the Jew as world-parasite. Coming from the Near East, he has spread over the entire world through the centuries, not as a harmless soul, but race-conscious and driven to fulfill the commandment of his god Yahweh, to fulfill the old dream and promise of world domination. His path to success has been long and rarely smooth. Time and again, Judaism was thrown back, but always it gathered itself again and began anew towards its goal. The races and nations, however, who did not defend themselves fittingly against this parasite remain scattered and broken along its path. And along with them, the forsaken creations of their genius and artistry, drained, twisted, or devoured by the same Jews: the decayed or diseased bodies of the victims, destroyed by the parasites, who in the meantime look around anxiously for new hosts.

# THE IDEA OF JEWISH WORLD SUPREMACY

### 46. Striving for world dominion is a religious duty for the Jew

It is now easy to see that Judaism, in its planned dispersion across the world, had no intention of establishing itself more or less firmly in one state or another, but that all of these bastions were only intended to serve in the final advance toward world domination. The doctrines of the Talmud not only gave the Jew the right to rule this world, but even imposed the achievement of world supremacy as a duty given to him by his God.

At all times, the Jews tried to conceal this goal as much as possible. Their centuries of experience told them that in the long run, no healthy race, or even more generally the collective races of the Earth, would ever leave such a goal unchallenged. This is one reason why the Jews were also so reluctant to make the Talmud available in good translations to a broad non-Jewish public. But wherever their goals for achieving world dominion became apparent too early, their strategy throughout history was to deny everything, or to present the claim as a statement by someone not to be taken seriously.

All the same, it was a Jew as influential as Walther Rathenau who wrote the following sentences in an essay in the Christmas edition of the Vienna newspaper *Neue Freie Presse* in 1909:

> Three hundred men, each of whom knows the others, direct the economic fortunes of the continent, and seek successors from their own environs. The strange causes of this strange phenomenon, which throws a glimmer into the darkness of future social development, are not under consideration here.

Rathenau himself later said that of all the statements he made, this one later caused him the greatest difficulties. No matter what we want to make from these lines of Rathenau, one thing is certain: Something here resonates about the methodology that Judaism is to use to achieve world dominion. The social development that Rathenau is hinting at is, as the Führer once put it, that of *tyrannical capitalism.*

## 47. Jewish world supremacy would form a tyrannical slave state

By no means would Jewish world dominion be a world government of justice and equality, or the solution to social difficulties. Rather, according to the doctrines of Jewish law, the entire non-Jewish world would be exploited, tyrannized, enslaved, and thrown back into the darkest state of deprivation by Judaism, the effects of which can hardly be imagined given our current circumstances. The fate of Russia provides at least an approximate example, and it is therefore no coincidence that the Jews placed the greatest hope in the possibilities of the Russian region, with its vast human and natural resources, as a springboard for achieving their goals.

We read in the Midrash Talpiyot how Judaism foresees its domination over the non-Jews:

> God created the non-Jews, although they are the same as animals, in the form of humans... However, he created them, for no other purpose than that they serve the Jews day and night and never abandon this service. It is not appropriate for Jews to be served by animals in the form of animals, but rather by animals in the form of humans.

Talmud Tractate Bava Batra 54b2 states: "The belongings of the non-Jews are like the desert, and whoever takes possession of them first acquires them." Berakhot 35b7 states: "As long as the Jews fulfill the will of Yahweh, their work will be done by the hands of others." And finally, the Tractate Soferim 15,10 says: "The most proven means of achieving world supremacy over all the races is to kill the best of the non-Jews".[38]

## 48. The Protocols of the Elders of Zion

At this point we should also consider the Protocols of the Elders of Zion, which exposes the Jewish conspiracy for world domination, and which

---

[38] See also Midrash Tanchuma, Beschalach 8,1.

can be seen as the General Staff plan of Judaism. This work details for Jews the plot to penetrate into the bloodstreams and organs of the non-Jewish peoples; it is the recipe for how non-Jewish states are to be undermined in order to deliver them completely into the hands of the Jewish parasites.

With control over gold and the press, through inciting the workers and provoking the social classes against each other, by disenfranchising the landowners, fomenting war and inciting the population, through opposing religious sentiment and eliminating the non-Jewish intelligentsia and the non-Jewish state order, the non-Jewish world will be unhinged so that Jewish world supremacy and a regime of terror can be unleashed.

Here are some passages from this Jewish plan:

- "For this reason, we must not hesitate at bribery, fraud, and treason when these can help us to reach our end." (Protocol #1)
- "These things are necessary to maintain a terror that induces blind submission." (Protocol #1)
- "Thanks to the press, we have gathered gold in our hands, although it cost us rivers of blood and tears." (Protocol #2)
- "Out of governments, we made arenas on which party wars are fought out. Soon, chaos and bankruptcy will appear everywhere." (Protocol #3)
- "These simple-minded and ignorant masses will gladly shed the blood of those of whom they have hated since childhood and whose property they will then be able to loot." (Protocol #3)
- "To control public opinion, it is necessary to perplex it by the expression of numerous contradictory opinions…" (Protocol #5)
- "In lieu of modern rulers, we will place a monstrosity—a monstrosity called the Super-Governmental Administration." (Protocol #5)
- "We will shatter the Goy family and its educational importance. (Protocol #10)
- "God has scattered us, his Chosen People, and in this dispersal, which seemed to the world to be our weakness, has proved to be our strength. This has now brought us to the

threshold of universal rule. Little remains to be built on these
foundations." (Protocol #11)[39]

It goes without saying that the Protocols should be viewed as a Jewish
cryptogram. For world Jewry, the revelation of the Protocols among the
non-Jewish peoples was a major political catastrophe. The Jews, therefore, tried to challenge the authenticity of the Protocols using every possible means of distortion and falsification. A useless effort; it is possible
from the mere consideration of world political events to demonstrate that
Judaism has strictly followed the instructions of the Protocols. The whole
of Jewish literature contains countless mosaic stones from which the image of the Protocols can be assembled, and conclusive evidence can be
provided for the authenticity of this Jewish world conspiracy.

But the spirit of the Talmud also wafts towards us from the Protocols; from it we hear the Zohar;[40] it contains the filthy passages from the
Old Testament of Judaism in a slightly different form. So the Protocols,
in their basic foundation, are the product of Jewish thought across the
ages. They took shape after world Jewry felt strong enough to organize
itself politically, around the same time as the founding of the first global
Jewish organization, the Alliance Israélite Universelle. At the beginning
of the 1860s, Mordecai (Karl Marx) appeared as the apostle of the class
struggle. And a few years later, the entire civilized world took notice of
the Paris Commune.

The founder of the Alliance Israélite Universelle, the Jew Adolphe
Crémieux, French Minister of Justice, is a friend of Karl Marx and Prime
Minister Gambetta; he is also the Grand Master of the Grand Orient de
France lodge of freemasons.

The French writer Maurice Joly—perhaps also of Jewish descent—
belongs to this Masonic rotary as well. At this time, Joly wrote a small
brochure, which must have given the impression at first glance that it was
directed against the French regime of the time. In all likelihood, it was
only comprehensible to the initiated among the Jews, and already it in-
cluded a significant part of the Protocols. The founder of the World Zionist Organization, Theodor Herzl, alludes to such connections in his novel

---

[39] All passages taken from *Protocols of the Elders of Zion: The Definitive English Edition* (2023; Clemens & Blair).
[40] The Zohar is a work of Jewish Kabbalah.

*The Old New Land*. There is no doubt that such ideas, once so clearly expressed, would continue to have an effect and were further developed within small Jewish circles, but also within Freemasonry.

Nothing is more natural than to assume that Maurice Joly was inspired by his great revolutionary Jewish friends. After the world center of international Judaism shifted to London, the First Zionist World Congress took place in Basel in 1897. From this point on, Judaism, which became increasingly powerful and more fully developed, displayed an activity that was bound to attract the attention of the non-Jewish world. The boldest political demands became now more and more numerous in Jewish literature, and Jewish megalomania and arrogance became increasingly clear. Conscious of imminent victory over the non-Jews, people sometimes quite carelessly spilled the beans.

### 49. The Jews' deficit of creativity

Now, it's astonishing to recognize that the Jews have absolutely no clear idea about the practical form they want for their world dominion. Rosenberg rightly points out in his *Myth of the 20th Century* that a romantic idea of this world empire prevailed in the writings of Judaism. He writes:

> In the entire Old Testament, we find no trace of belief in immortality, unless it be the reflection of the proven outward effect of the Persians on the Jews during the banishment.
>
> The Jewish aim is the creation of a paradise on Earth. For this purpose, as is stated in the later holy books, "the righteous" (that is, the Jews) will creep into the Promised Land from their graves all over the world, emerging through holes bored in the Earth by unknown forces solely for them. The Targum, the Midrashim, and the Talmud describe with delight this magnificent state of affairs in the expected paradise. The Chosen People will then rule over the entire world. All other peoples will become its slaves. They will die and be born again in order to go anew to hell. The Jews, however, will not go there, but will lead a blessed life on Earth.

Jerusalem will be rebuilt in the most splendid way. The sabbath boundaries will be set with jewels and pearls. If anyone should have debts to pay, then he will need only tear a pearl from the hedge and he will become free of all obligations. Fruit will ripen every month, grapes will grow as large as an entire room, grain will grow of its own accord, the wind will blow the corn together, and the Jews will only need to shovel up the meal. Eight hundred varieties of roses will grow in the gardens, and streams of milk, balsam, honey, and wine will flow through Palestine. Every Jew will possess a tent over which a golden vine will grow on which 30 pearls will hang. Under every vine will stand a table with jewels. In this paradise, 800 kinds of flowers will bloom. In the midst, the Tree of Life will grow, radiating 500,000 kinds of taste and scent. Seven clouds will lie over the tree, and the Jews will tap its branches so that its magnificent perfume is wafted from one end of the world to the other.

This land of milk and honey grew with religious sanction and then celebrated its rebirth in Jewish Marxism, with its splendid future state. Jewish greed exists because of their bankrupt theology, whether of the past or present. At the same time, they almost completely lack a truly spiritual and artistic creativity. The primary religious element is lacking. The outward belief in immortality has been given only a superficial adjustment to an essentially alien outlook. It has never been an inwardly-determined driving force.[41]

Aside from materialistic wishful thinking, this idea shows a lack of genuine substantive creative aptitude by the Jews. His field is purely material and organizational activity. This is where they display their innate computational talents. A German creative personality is something foreign and incomprehensible to Judaism and therefore something deeply hated because of the awareness of inferiority.

---

[41] *Myth*, pp. 251-252.

## 50. The Alliance Israélite Universelle

This uncertainty on the part of the Jews, however, in no way prevented them from making the most diverse preparations for the task they had in mind. Thus, as mentioned, the Jew Isaac Adolphe Crémieux (1796-1880) founded the Alliance Israélite Universelle, whose first annual meeting took place on 31 May 1861. The following lines, which Crémieux wrote that year, serve to characterize this organization precisely, which is superficially disguised as an association for the protection of Jewish rights: "The Nationalities should disappear! Religions should perish! But Israel will not stop, for this little nation is the chosen people of God."

Anticipating the dream of Jewish victory, the Zionist leader Theodor Herzl (1860-1904) wrote in his diary on July 10/11, 1895: "Yes, we have become a scourge for the peoples who once tormented us."

## 51. Jewish world supremacy would be the end of the world

Another organization devised for the implementation of Jewish plans is the aforementioned Freemasonry. Here too, the mask of a charitable welfare institution is repeatedly emphasized as a camouflage, while we have established through research and further experience that the World Masonic Organization is nothing other than a Jewish tool. It is pointless at the present time to consider whether one or another person in this world became, and was more or less consciously, a Freemason. Moreover, it is important to recognize that Freemasonry or similar institutions must never exist again, neither in Germany nor in Europe, if the peoples of Europe do not want to contribute to their own misfortune and destruction.

We have already identified the role that followers of Marxism and the religious denominations often played as unconscious helpers of Judaism. But if we now see how the Jew strived, from all sides and in all areas of life, to hollow out not only our race, but all the peoples of the world, to parasitically drain them and make them the playthings of his plans for world supremacy, then we must recognize that the Jewish danger is the greatest we could ever encounter.

We draw the conclusion from this that the very existence of the idea of Jewish world supremacy is a danger, that the possibility of Jewish world domination is a special threat to all peoples, and that the implementation of Jewish world mastery would be the end of the peoples and races; it would also mean the end of that world which is connected with the works of our entire culture, with the consciousness of our entire history, and with the essence of our blood heritage in general.

# — 6 —
# THE NATIONAL SOCIALIST FIGHT AGAINST THE JEWISH WORLD-PARASITE

### 52. "By resisting the Jews, I am fighting for the work of the Lord"

Despite all the struggles of Judaism, it has not truly succeeded in alienating the German people from their inner essence. The German people owe this especially to their leader Adolf Hitler. His decades-long struggle has enabled tens, even hundreds of thousands of Germans to gain insight every year. They did not become anti-Semites in the old sense, no matter how grateful the German people must be to the old political pioneers; rather, Hitler's followers became fervent opponents of Jewish influence and fighters for a just German standard of life.

It had a liberating effect on the German people when, during the announcement of the party program, the phrases were uttered that no Jew may be a comrade of the people, that the common good must take precedence over self-interest—in short, that the Jewish spirit in us and around us must be vigorously combatted.

The realization that Judaism was the greatest enemy of the German people prompted the Führer to take up the fight against this enemy with relentless ferocity. From the beginning, the Jews saw him as the one who would become the most dangerous to them. They fought him with every means at their disposal: through the press, economically, through lies and deceit, through attempts to incite their own people, and finally inciting the entire world against him and his people. Since the leader showed no personal consideration whatsoever and completely ignored his own well-being, their plans have not yet succeeded and will never succeed.

The Jews tried to harm the NSDAP where they could. They didn't even shy away from murder. When we think of Wilhelm Gustloff, who was murdered by the Jew David Frankfurter in Davos on 4 February 1936, two statements are worth remembering. Frankfurter said: "I committed the crime because I am Jewish." And the Führer said on February 12, in Schwerin:

This is no coincidence, there is a guiding hand that organized these crimes and wants to continue to organize them.
This time, the person responsible for these acts has now actually emerged. For the first time, some harmless German
comrade is not being duped. It is a credit to both Switzerland and our own Germans in Switzerland that no one allowed themselves to be persuaded to commit this crime, so
that the spiritual mastermind himself had to become the
perpetrator. Wilhelm Gustloff has been felled by the power
that is waging a fanatical fight, not only against our German people.

We also remember the murder of Counselor vom Rath on 7 November
1938 by the Jew Herschel Grünspan in Paris. But we especially remember all the murders that were committed against our party and like-
minded comrades during the fighting, either by the Jews themselves or
instigated by them. Hundreds of our party comrades fell victim to these
assassination attempts. Their deaths have become unified in the sacrifice
of Horst Wessel, a symbol of our National Socialist time of struggle.[42]

But let us also think of the *spiritual* murder that the Jews tried to
commit against hundreds of thousands of Germans at that time:

With every means of chicanery, agitation, blackmail, and exploitation of their disposal at the time, they tried to prevent Germans who were
becoming conscious of their German identity from joining the Führer's
movement. It is always important for us to remember how many of the
old party comrades not only gave up their occupations out of loyalty to
the leader and the idea, but in many cases also lost their entire old way of
life and their so-called bourgeois respectability, and preferred to take
everything upon themselves, rather than to give in to the wheedling and
debasement of Judaism. It was their steadfastness and loyalty, their un-
wavering belief in the justice of their cause and their faith in victory, that
had an exemplary effect on millions of their fellow citizens.

Individual numbers may indicate how strong Judaism was in Germany in terms of numbers alone. In 1933 there were still over 500,000

---

[42] Wessel was leader in the SA who was killed by communist assassins in February 1930. Four people were eventually convicted and executed for the murder, including a Jewess, Sally Epstein.

religious Jews living in the country. This does not include all the many Jews who adopted a different, mostly Christian, denomination for reasons of camouflage. Over 160,000 religious Jews lived in Berlin alone. The proportion of Jews taking emergency funds was 56 percent—52 percent among health insurance fund doctors, 48 percent among lawyers, and 42 percent among doctors in general. Jews went bankrupt twenty times as frequently as Germans, all converted to the actual percentage of their share in German national life. With regard to the natural law of our struggle against Judaism, we agree with Reichsführer SS Heinrich Himmler, who wrote the following in his small work "The SS as Anti-Bolshevist Combat Organization":

> We consider it right to maintain that, so long as there are men on the Earth, the battle between man and the subhuman is a historical rule, that this battle conducted by the Jew against the nations, as far into the past as we can look, belongs to the natural course of life on our planet. One can safely come to the conviction that this life-and-death struggle is perhaps even as much a natural law as the battle of man against any epidemic, as the battle of the plague bacillus against the healthy body.[43]

With the struggle of this current war launched against us by world Jewry, our fight against the Jews has entered a decisive stage. As Rosenberg said in his speech on 22 June 1943:

> The alliance between world democracy, world Bolshevism, and world Jewry, which many do not want to admit, has today become a direct political fact and a military threat. It is therefore perhaps not superfluous to point out now that this realization was a fundamental insight of the National Socialist worldview. I may therefore quote a few words that I published in the magazine *World Struggle* under the title "Jewish World Politics" in June 1924. It reads: "Many politicians who are still moving in old ways of thinking will

---

[43] From *Classic Essays on the Jewish Question* (2022), p. 243.

say it is wrong to mention 'anti-capitalist' Marxism and capitalist democracy in the same breath, but any deeper look shows that both phenomena represent the same worldview: they form the precipitate of the age of monetary rule."

After describing the financial development, he then goes on to say:

Nothing characterizes the obvious decline of a world age more than the fact that the former explorers, conquerors—in short, the masters—stepped down and made way for the mediator, the trader, and the servant. The path leads from individual conquerors, then to consolidated dynastic power states, and finally to plutocratic parliamentary democracy.

Regarding the end of the world war, he states:

The most magnificent monuments of ancient European culture are irretrievably gone. An unspeakable calamity afflicts hundreds of millions. But no people have become free. Neither the betrayed nor the defeated, neither the victors nor their satellites, have won the war—although the field grays, Poilus and Tommys, believed they were fighting for the freedom and the world-standing of their nations, and this idea gave them the strength to fight. They have all been shamefully deceived before the battle began, although only today are a few beginning to open their eyes.

After explaining that the Bolshevik leaders traveled to Russia from ghettos all over the world in order to push forward the revolution there, which was initially democratic, Rosenberg then says:

Germany owes the victory of the Bolshevik revolution in the East primarily to the revolt of 9 November 1918. From it follow today's consequences. By recognizing Soviet Judea, England has infested its own house with termites. In France, the Jew Léon Blum and his backers are putting together a force that is ready to attack if the *bloc national* is no longer

viable and usable. This is the current alliance in Europe: the
stock exchanges of London, Paris, and Moscow. Constrict-
ed by this political pressure, the gentlemen—as long as
they are non-Jews—breathe in Berlin and Rome.

The following was proclaimed as the National Socialist thesis at the time:

But out of the chaos, out of the shame, the national ideal
confronted the international idea. The victory of this ideal
in all areas of life entails the real-world revolution of the
20th century. ... We are not dreamers and do not preach
'world peace' and eternal international brotherhood. But no
matter what the future may bring, we strive for the victory
of an aristocratic ideal over the greasy merchant spirit of
today's passing age. This is the world struggle of today, the
world revolution of tomorrow, the war which we do not
know when it will be over, but which must be fought through
if Germany and the whole of the old Europe are not to de-
cay in the mire like so many of the races of ancient history.

I believe these words, written almost 20 years ago, express exactly the
struggle of powers that has once again coalesced and now stand opposing
each other in the decisive world conflict and war. On the side of the entire enemy coalition are the wing states of the USA and the Soviet Union.
Every European must account for the nature of these two groups.

This struggle forces us to make our own fundamental personal decisions. True to the demands of the party program, every single German
must constantly re-examine himself to ensure that he also eliminates the
last vestiges of decades of unhindered Jewish infiltration. He must put
aside materialistic and self-centered thought and action, down to the
smallest things in everyday life. He must help to see correctly the facts of
a controlled economy and to eliminate all remnants of capitalistic and
Marxist thinking. He must see work as the highest value and the basic
concept of the German economy, and must return money to a serving
roll. He must not separate the ideological-political realm from the economic realm. Perhaps the liberal can do that, but the National Socialist
must see a unified whole. He must at all times recognize the fateful ne-

cessity of our struggle against our enemy controlled by Judaism, and against Judaism itself, and be consciously aware of these facts.

He must therefore assume a maximum of personal responsibility and must serve the movement and the state as much as he can. He must not just give lip service to the term 'fellowship of the people', but must live it in practice. He is not allowed to make demands on others in the intellectual and cultural areas that he himself will not or cannot keep. He must not sneer at folk art, folk music, or folk dance and customs, because they are perceived as outdated or unfashionable in the wake of Jewish parasitic cultural distortion, but he must do his part to revive all these things. He must not attach himself to things in the intellectual life of our people that cannot be reconciled with the National Socialist demands of the future.

In the field of racial policy, he must not affirm the demands of our movement in general, only to subsequently not be an abiding combat-ready, self-sacrificing, and enthusiastic comrade-in-arms—one who, im-bued with our duties, wants to preserve the inner freedom of the German people, and who finally fully understands the magnitude of the destiny that Providence has assigned us to fulfill in our living space.

The fulfillment of all these demands is, for each and every one of us, the best, safest, and most effective means of combating Judaism in general and against the parasitic nature of the Jew in particular. For it is only the unity of our *national body* and our *racial will* that closes off any possibility for the Jews to penetrate further into our national life. The Jew must then realize that he can neither return to Germany, nor can he again take spiritual possession of us.

And finally, such a close and united attitude of the German people is the best guarantee that other races will recognize—not only from our struggle, but from our new attitude—that we are on the right path and they are still on the wrong path.

The Führer says: "By resisting the Jew, I am fighting for the work of the Lord".[44] Just as he gave us the model for the fight against Judaism, the German people have the same duty in reality far and wide: *through the example of a determined struggle against the Jewish world-parasite!*

---

[44] *Mein Kampf*, vol. 1, sec. 2.27, p. 98.

# BIBLIOGRAPHY

Bischoff, E. 2023. *The Book of the Shulchan Aruch*. Clemens & Blair.

Chamberlain, H. 1899/1968. *Foundations of the Nineteenth Century*. H. Fertig.

Dalton, T. 2019. *The Jewish Hand in the World Wars*. Castle Hill.

Dalton, T. 2020. *Debating the Holocaust: A New Look at Both Sides* (4th ed.). Castle Hill.

Dalton, T. 2020. *Eternal Strangers: Critical Views of Jews and Judaism*. Castle Hill.

Dalton, T. (ed.) 2022. *Classic Essays on the Jewish Question: 1850 to 1945*. Clemens & Blair.

Dalton, T. (ed.) 2023. *Protocols of the Elders of Zion: The Definitive English Edition*. Clemens & Blair.

Goebbels, J. 2019. *Goebbels on the Jews*. Castle Hill.

Hitler, A. 2019. *Hitler on the Jews*. Castle Hill.

Hitler, A. 2022. *Mein Kampf: A New English Translation* (2 volumes). Clemens & Blair.

Luther, M. 2020. *On the Jews and their Lies*. Clemens & Blair.

Mommsen, T. 1856/1871. *The History of Rome* (vol. 4). Scribner.

Penman, R. 2021. *Pan-Judah! Political Cartoons of Der Stürmer, 1925-1945*. Clemens & Blair.

Penman, R. 2022. *Pan-Judah! Volume Two*. Clemens & Blair.

Rosenberg, A. 1920/2020. *The Track of the Jew through the Ages* (A. Jacobs, trans.) Ostara.

Rosenberg, A. 2021. *The Myth of the 20th Century* (T. Dalton, ed.). Clemens & Blair.